FRUSTRATED

The three children of Edmund of Langley, first Duke of York.

Brian Wainwright

Published internationally by Brian Wainwright

CONTENTS

AUTHOR'S NOTE

My interest in the early years of the House of York was kindled many years ago, and eventually led to my writing a novel *Within the Fetterlock* which was based around the life of Constance of York, but which also naturally includes the other members of her family, and in particular the fascinating and slippery Edward, 2nd Duke of York.

This little book is intended to assemble the facts about Edward of Langley's three children, each of whom is well worth further study. Unlike some writers of fiction, I do not pretend to be a professional historian, and this work is intended primarily for the general reader of history rather than the academic. Nonetheless, it is my hope that it may encourage someone better qualified than I am to undertake a more advanced study of these characters. They have generally been given a harsh deal by historians. Edward's importance in the reigns of both Richard II and Henry IV tends to be neglected. Writers of fiction, like Georgette Heyer in *My Lord John,* frequently depict him as an amiable buffoon. He was, I think, rather more than that. Historians, where they mention her at all, tend to be dismissive of Constance, often describing her in sexist terms that say more about themselves than their subject, or even suggesting she was insane. As for Richard of Conisbrough, it must be admitted that the known facts about him are few and far between, while the Southampton Conspiracy, as it is presented to us, makes no real sense at all.

The lives of the three siblings touched upon one another, and so some repetition is unavoidable. I hope it does not prove too tedious for the reader, but it means that each short biography can be read in isolation.

I have included a list of my principal sources, although this does not include all the many and various works I have consulted in my pursuit of Constance and her brothers. For anyone wanting to know more, and in particular more details of the Southampton Plot, I strongly recommend *Henry V and the Southampton Plot* by T.B. Pugh, which despite its title contains more within its covers about these three people than any other single volume. I do not always agree with Pugh's conclusions, but as a source of facts the book is difficult to criticise.

Edmund of Langley's principal cognizance was a falcon within a fetterlock. Chosen, it is said, because he was shut out from any hope of the throne by his elder brothers and their children. Be that as it may, from 1461, with the accession of Edward IV, the fetterlock was depicted as open. The House of York was no longer confined by it – the falcon could fly free.

HISTORICAL BACKGROUND

This book covers an era that runs from the last years of Edward III to the early years of Henry V. Readers who have not studied this period in detail need to have at least the bare bones of the political background to these three lives.

By the 1370s, Edward III's battlefield successes were a memory. The English had been driven back from most of the French conquests, and their military interventions in France all ended in expensive failure. The country was close to bankruptcy and French raids on the English coast became more and more prevalent. The possibility of a French invasion was all too real.

By the end of his reign Edward was senile. Of his three remaining sons, John of Gaunt, Duke of Lancaster, was by far the most experienced in politics, war and diplomacy but it is hard to exaggerate his unpopularity. This was the legacy Richard II inherited when he became King of England at the age of 10.

Richard was not the pacifist some have thought him, nor was he a weakling, nor yet a physical coward. His actions at the time of the Peasants Revolt, 1381, when he was only 14, should stamp on that last libel. However, he came to see that the war with France was unsustainable, and beyond England's ability to finance. (The Peasants Revolt had been caused by novel taxation that arose from the financial crisis.)

Although this policy was broadly supported by the Duke of Lancaster, it cannot be said that it was popular. Many of the nobles and gentry saw the potential of personal profit in the war, while others thought that seeking peace was a betrayal of the national honour. Richard's personal rule also caused problems. He preferred a narrow clique of advisers, and some of his nobles felt themselves unjustly excluded from power. It is sometimes said he gave too much heed to the young and the low-born. This does not stand up to serious scrutiny. Most of his advisers were men of mature years, and the much-abused 'favourite', Robert de Vere, Earl of Oxford and later Duke of Ireland, was the head of one of the oldest magnate families in England, albeit not one of the richest.

The young Richard was also prone to irrational and impulsive behaviour. On one occasion he leapt from one boat to another in the middle of the Thames in order to threaten the Archbishop of Canterbury with his sword. On another, on hearing a rumour of a plot, he ordered the summary execution of the Duke of Lancaster. Fortunately, in both cases, wiser counsel prevailed and the King calmed down.

During Gaunt's absence in Castile, powerful opposition grew against the King's advisers, led by the Duke of Gloucester and the earls of Arundel and Warwick. These men were later joined by Gaunt's son, Henry Bolingbroke, Earl of Derby and Arundel's son-in-law, Thomas Mowbray, Earl Marshal. An armed coup was undertaken against the King's Government, and the opposition, known as the Lords Appellant, held a Parliament which executed or banished most of the King's ministers and supporters.

Richard regained control in a peaceful coup of his own. Shortly afterwards Gaunt returned to England and added his support. Relations between the King and his eldest surviving uncle had hitherto been strained – now they became cordial. Richard ruled for some years with moderation. He neither recalled his exiled friends nor punished the Appellants. He did, however, begin to build his own party of supporters, this time one which was dominated by men who were close to him in blood and undeniably aristocratic.

Richard pursued his policy of peace with France, and in 1396 a 28 year truce was agreed. The next year he took his revenge against Gloucester, Arundel and Warwick – Bolingbroke and Mowbray having by this time switched sides.

In 1398 Bolingbroke and Mowbray quarrelled, each effectively accusing the other of high treason. This led to the famous abortive duel at Gosford Green near Coventry, after which both men were banished, Mowbray for life. The following year, after Gaunt died, Richard forfeited their lands and made Bolingbroke's banishment permanent. However, it does appear that he intended to restore the Lancastrian inheritance at some point as the grants of Bolingbroke's land were made with the restriction, 'until Henry, Duke of Lancaster shall sue for the same.' Moreover, Richard gave his exiled cousin ample funding, including £1,500 just weeks before Bolingbroke invaded.

With Richard and most of his supporters absent in Ireland, Henry Bolingbroke landed in Yorkshire and overcame opposition with scarcely a blow struck. Richard returned with his army, but abandoned his main force in South Wales, only to find that his other contingent, sent to North Wales, had disbanded. He surrendered and was forced to abdicate, as well as being deposed by Parliament.

Bolingbroke now became King Henry IV. He defeated Richard's noble supporters when they rose against him early in 1400, but that was far from the end of his troubles. Although Richard died, probably murdered, at Pontefract in February 1400, many people still believed he was still alive and living in Scotland and sought to restore him, while others supported the claim of the young Earl of March. Wales rose in revolt under Owain Glyndŵr and soon Henry found himself involved in conflict in Gascony, Scotland and Ireland as well, quite apart from the various internal rebellions he had to deal with in England itself.

Henry's finances were in dire straits for most of his reign, and his own health worsened from about 1405 onwards, with the Prince of Wales acting as virtual regent at certain times. However, in his last days, Henry was able to amuse himself by interfering in the internal politics of France, and the great debate centred on whether to support the Burgundian or the Armagnac faction.

Bolingbroke's death in 1413 was followed by the accession of his eldest son, Henry of Monmouth, as Henry V. The new King's regime was unstable at first, though he made a serious attempt to pacify the remaining dissidents, offering a pardon to Glyndŵr, allowing Henry Percy, Earl of Northumberland, home from Scottish exile and translating Richard II's remains from an obscure tomb at Kings Langley to Westminster Abbey. He was nonetheless faced with a serious Lollard rising in 1414, led by Sir John Oldcastle, and then by the Southampton Plot of 1415.

His subsequent victories in France stabilised the Lancastrian regime. He died in 1422, and no one can say with certainty whether or not his achievements in France would have been sustainable had he lived longer.

THE PARENTS

Edmund of Langley, born on 5th June 1341, was the fourth surviving son of King Edward III and his Queen, Philippa of Hainault. It is hard to argue against the view that he was the least important and least effective of Edward's five legitimate sons, but in Edmund's defence it must be stated that he was never given an adequate endowment of land. For the English nobility of this time, and for many years after, land was the principal source of wealth, and power was, as always, based on possession of wealth. Whatever personal qualities Edmund may or may not have possessed, he never acquired the financial 'kick' that was imperative for success in high politics.

One factor in Edmund's relative poverty was that he was the only one of his brothers not to marry an heiress. Instead he was given as his wife Isabella of Castile, who was even poorer than he was himself. Typically, his thrusting elder brother, John of Gaunt, secured the heiress to the Castilian throne, Constance, for himself, and it was arranged that Edmund should marry her younger sister, just to avert any possibility of the inheritance escaping from the family. It appears that Isabella had little but her clothes and a few jewels – she and her sister were exiled, their father's throne having been usurped by an illegitimate brother. Edmund and Isabella were required to renounce all claim to the Castilian throne in favour of John of Gaunt and Constance. It is not apparent that they received any significant compensation for this sacrifice. Although Gaunt's attempts to take over Castile by military force eventually failed, and at heavy cost in both treasure and blood, he did achieve a settlement by which his daughter by Constance, Catherine or Catalina of Lancaster, was married to the usurper's heir and eventually became Queen of Castile. In addition he received a very substantial indemnity and a pension for life. He did not choose to share this largesse with his younger brother, who had been required to accept a disadvantageous marriage in the pursuit of Gaunt's interests.

In the treaty between Gaunt and his rival Edmund and Isabella were not even mentioned.

It does not appear to have been a particularly happy marriage. The Chronicler Walsingham, albeit not the kindest or least biased of judges, says that Isabella was 'a worldly and sensuous woman' although he was careful to add that she repented her bad ways before she died.

Edmund was created Duke of York by Richard II in 1385. His younger brother, Thomas of Woodstock, was made Duke of Gloucester on the same day.

Isabella died on 23 December 1392, and not many months later (one uncertain source gives November 1393) he married Joan (or Joanne) Holland, one of the daughters of the King's half-brother, Thomas Holland, Earl of Kent. (Kent seems to have had a policy of marrying his daughters to all the leading families – the eldest, Alianore, was married to the Earl of March (at this point heir to the throne) while later on Joanne's younger sister, Margaret, was married to Gaunt's son, John Beaufort, Earl of Somerset.) Joanne was very young at the time of her wedding to Langley and was to outlive him by many years – and go through three more husbands in the process.

According to Froissart, writing in the middle 90s, Edmund was extremely attached to his young and beautiful wife and had little thought for anything else. The chronicler Hardyng states that the Duke of York was more interested in hawking and hunting than in politics. We might be excused, therefore, for thinking of Edmund as living the life of a very grand country squire with a consort who was younger than his own daughter. The truth is however that York spent much of his time at Richard's Court, and frequently attended Councils and witnessed Charters.

York was a moderate in politics. At the time of the Appellant crisis, he actually stood up in Parliament and challenged his brother Gloucester to mortal combat over the case of Sir Simon Burley, whom the Appellants wished to execute. On the other hand, he seems to have had sympathy for Henry Bolingbroke when the latter was banished, and the resistance he offered to Henry's invasion was feeble at best. However, by this stage of his life he was almost certainly not in the best of health. Examination of his skeleton in the 19th Century revealed several wounds that must have given great pain. The *Complete Peerage* suggests he was 'crippled in later life'. Although he supported Henry IV in the early months of the new reign, less and less is heard of him until his death on 1 August 1402.

SON AND HEIR

Edward of York, Earl of Rutland and Cork, Duke of Aumale and second Duke of York

Edward was born in early 1373. He is sometimes known to historians as 'Edward of Norwich' but as his parents had no direct connection with that city it seems likely to me that this is a misreading of the Norman-French version of Edward of York, Edward 'd'Everwyk'. Having said that, it is far from clear where Edmund of Langley's two elder children were born. Some hopeful genealogists are happy to pronounce that they came into the world at Conisbrough, but this is not recorded and must be reckoned as pure guesswork. The family's later 'headquarters', Fotheringhay Castle, was not in Edmund of Langley's possession at the time of their arrival, so it's unlikely they were born there. On balance, the safest verdict is – place of birth unknown.

Edward was knighted at the coronation of King Richard II on 16 July 1377, when only four years old and clearly too young to be a knight in more than name. He was of course one of King Richard's (very many) first cousins, but the honour demonstrates that knighthood was no longer something won by merit, or even following years of training, but could simply be bestowed on someone in recognition of their high birth.

He accompanied his parents to Portugal in 1381, and at Lisbon was married to the Infanta Beatriz, heir to the Portuguese crown. This marriage (more in the way of a betrothal given the ages of the couple) was swiftly annulled after the collapse of the English position in Portugal, and Beatriz married to Juan of Castile instead.

In 1387 Edward was appointed a Knight of the Garter. Richard II was having serious political difficulties at this time and this may be seen as one of a number of gestures to Edmund of Langley to reward him for his support. Edward's rewards from the Crown began to multiply as he himself secured the favour of his cousin the King.

On 22 January 1390 he was made Steward of Bury St. Edmunds, and the next month was created Earl of Rutland, with a grant of the town, castle and lordship of Oakham, the Forest of Rutland and shrievalty of that county. These grants were given for the term of his father's life, but Edward was in reality to use the title Earl of Rutland until his own death.

In January 1391, jointly with his parents, he received the reversion of the Keepership of the Forest of Bradon, Wiltshire. He was Admiral of the North from 22 March 1391, and Admiral of both North and West from 29 November (effectively Admiral of England) a post he retained until May 1398. As early as 1392, while still under age, he was serving on the King's Council.

In February 1392, he undertook the first of several diplomatic missions, as one of the commissioners to treat for a truce with France. He accompanied Richard II to Ireland in 1394, and took a prominent part in the military activity there. Edward's independent role included leading strike forces which burned villages and rounded up cattle as part of a strategy to deny resources to the King's opponents. This led to the submissions of a number of Gaelic chiefs from January 1395 onwards. Richard's success in Ireland is rarely recognised by historians, and Edward's part in the victory is even more overlooked.

During his time in Ireland, Edward acquired the title Earl of Cork. It was another sign of Richard II's favour, but would have brought little in the way of additional revenues.

On 28 May 1395 Edward became one of three feoffees (trustees) of the former dower lands of the late Queen Anne. This gave him considerable additional powers of patronage. A few days later he was granted the Keepership of Brigstock Park, Northamptonshire. Then in July he was appointed as one of the ambassadors to treat with the French with regards to a proposed marriage between Richard II and Isabella, eldest daughter of King Charles VI of France. He was also authorised to treat for a marriage between himself and Isabella's younger sister, Jeanne. From round about this time he is frequently referred to in official documents as 'the King's brother' rather than the correct 'the King's kinsman'. It may be that this was done in anticipation of Edward's marriage to Jeanne. However, the practice continued long after it became clear that no such marriage was to take place, so it is probably correct to see it as a particular mark of royal favour.

From 11 September 1396 until April 1398 Edward served as Constable of Dover and Lord Warden of the Cinque Ports. On

30 November 1396 he was also given the office of Keeper of the Channel Islands for life. Between February and June 1397 he was sent on a diplomatic mission with Thomas Mowbray, the Earl Marshal, to France and to the Count Palatine. The latter visit was part of an attempt to persuade the Electors of the Holy Roman Empire to appoint Richard II as King of the Romans, and thus as effective heir to the Holy Roman Emperor. Richard was later told that his election failed because of doubts in Germany that he had full control of England. It was probably this, rather than any fresh plotting, that persuaded him to take action against his old enemies, his uncle, Thomas of Woodstock, Duke of Gloucester, Richard Fitzalan, Earl of Arundel and Thomas Beauchamp, Earl of Warwick.

In the interim, Edward was granted the Constableship of Carisbrooke Castle and the Lordship of the Isle of Wight for life. He was also made Warden of the New Forest and Justice in Eyre South of Trent. He was also employing a large number of masons and carpenters to build him a house outside Temple Bar, London, though it would seem this project was never completed.

The day after the arrest of the Duke of Gloucester (11 July) Edward was appointed Constable of England in his uncle's room. He then served as one of eight appellants – another being his brother-in-law, Thomas Despenser – at the Parliamentary trial of Gloucester, Arundel and Warwick. Though 'trial' is a generous word in this case, the proceedings were consciously modelled on those used in 1388 against the King's supporters.

Edward's support was rewarded by a generous grant of additional lands. In addition, he was made Duke of Aumale, the Aumale title having ancient connections with the rich lordship of Holderness, which had been among those taken from Gloucester and given to Edward. As if this was not enough, he was made Havenor of Devon and Cornwall in October 1397. He also became Constable of the Tower, having been granted the reversion in the previous April.

While Arundel was publicly beheaded, and Warwick sentenced to life imprisonment, the Duke of Gloucester had been conveyed to Calais. Here he was almost certainly privately executed, though natural causes cannot be entirely ruled out. It was later claimed that Mowbray, now Duke of Norfolk and in charge of Calais, had been hesitant in despatching Gloucester and Edward sent one of his squires over to ensure the deed was completed. This allegation was to put Edward in grave danger in 1400, by which time Gloucester's death had come to be regarded as murder.

In February 1398, Edward was made Keeper of Carlisle and Warden of the West March. This appointment must have stirred the jealousy of the Percy and Neville families, especially as he had no lands in the area. Indeed, even allowing for the fact that the long-term truce with France included Scotland as well, it is hard to see how Edward could have performed the duties of the Warden effectively. On 15 March of the same year he received the first of two commissions, joint with the Duke of Surrey to 'arrest and chastise all traitors' and deal with them on a summary basis following a simple examination of the fact. This was in effect an extension and clarification of his powers as Lord High Constable.

Edward was now near the zenith of his power. He had gathered together a substantial endowment of lands and a collection of offices that amounted almost to the keys to the kingdom. He had, at least in theory, power of life and death over his fellow-subjects, and there was no doubt that he stood high in the King's favour.

His marriage at around this time to Philippa Mohun is therefore the more surprising. She was the youngest daughter of the late Lord Mohun, and had been married to two previous husbands, Lord Fitzwalter and Sir John Golafre, but had produced no children by either. She was at least ten years older than Edward; some historians have suggested nearer twenty. Moreover, although she and her sisters were theoretically co-heiresses of their father, Lord Mohun of Dunster, her inheritance had already been spent. Her mother, Lady Mohun, had obtained a jointure in the whole of the Mohun lands as far back as 1369, and sold the reversion to the Luttrell family in 1376. She did have some dower interest in the Fitzwalter and Golafre lands, but this was for the term of her life only, and the manors could not become a permanent asset of the House of York.

Although Joan, Lady Mohun was apparently an influential figure at Court – the Appellants had banished her from it – the most likely explanation for Edward's marriage is that he fell in love with Philippa. The Despenser connection may also have played its part, as Philippa was first cousin to Elizabeth de Burghersh, mother of Edward's brother-in-law, Thomas

Despenser. The marriage had taken place before October 1398 because at that point Edward received a Plenary Indulgence from the Pope covering himself and his wife. Apart from this there is remarkably little early evidence of the marriage. Philippa is not recorded as having received robes as Duchess of Aumale to attend Henry IV's coronation, and she did not receive Garter robes as Edward's wife until 1408! There were to be no children of the marriage, and given Philippa's prior history this is not surprising.

On 11 August 1398 Edward was one of three persons granted custody of the lands of the late Earl of March, who had been killed in Ireland. On 17 September that year, in his role as Constable, he presided over the famous abortive duel between his cousin Henry Bolingbroke and Thomas Mowbray, Duke of Norfolk, who had fallen out and effectively accused one another of treason. If Bolingbroke's account is to be believed (and there is no particular reason why it should be, except that it has survived) Mowbray had placed Edward and his brother-in-law Thomas Despenser in separate political groups, with the later drawn to a faction that was seeking to destroy Bolingbroke's father. That there was court intrigue going on seems to be quite probable, but its exact nature is hard to discern. Despenser had had the judgement against his ancestors reversed at the Shrewsbury Parliament earlier that year, but its effect had been more theoretical than practical. He had quitclaimed the earls of March and Salisbury without any apparent fuss, and there is no indication that King Richard planned to allow him to recover land from the House of Lancaster; quite the contrary, in fact.

Perhaps, however, Edward was seen as a more moderate member of the King's coterie, inclined to support Lancaster and Bolingbroke against any threat. He was one of those who offered sureties for Bolingbroke – apparently none could be found for Norfolk. Whether Edward was in fact such an ally is more questionable. One somehow doubts he shed many tears when Henry and Norfolk were both banished. Only John of Gaunt himself was now a more powerful subject, and Gaunt, as it proved, did not have long to live.

On 20 March 1399 Edward was assigned a large part of the Lancastrian inheritance, after the death of Gaunt. He was later to claim that he drew no money from this – it is just possible he did not, as the time he held them was quite short. As with the other grants, the limitation was added 'until Henry, Duke of Lancaster, shall sue for the same.' Although Bolingbroke's exile had been extended to life, it does not appear King Richard intended permanently to alienate the Lancastrian inheritance. Indeed, he continued to send his exiled cousin large sums of cash for his maintenance. There was no question of Bolingbroke having to beg his bread in the gutter.

In his *Fears of Henry IV* Ian Mortimer suggests that at this point Edmund of Langley was heir to the throne, with Edward established as the most likely person to succeed Richard II. This may seem unlikely. However, the established heir to throne (if there was one) Roger Mortimer, Earl of March, had died under something of a cloud, and his sons were but young boys. Bolingbroke was banished for life, and his three Beaufort brothers had all been born illegitimate – though they were legitimised in 1397. Moreover, the Beauforts had no claim to most of the lands of the duchy of Lancaster, since these had come from Gaunt's first wife, Blanche of Lancaster.

There is also the little matter of the confession of Sir William Bagot, made after Bolingbroke took the throne. Bagot stated that King Richard had told him that he had wanted Edward to succeed him. Apparently Richard felt Edward was *the most able, wise and powerful man that he could think of.*

King Richard now departed to his second campaign in Ireland, taking with him the majority of his noble supporters, including Edward. (Edmund of Langley, Duke of York, was left behind as Keeper of England.)

Edward was late arriving at the muster, because he had been in the North in connection with his duties as Warden of the March. His delay was seen in retrospect as part of his treachery by hostile French chroniclers, but was almost certainly legitimate and authorised.

When word reached Ireland of Bolingbroke's landing in Yorkshire, Edward was supposedly the one who advised Richard II to split his forces, sending some to North Wales and some to South Wales. Again, this is often represented as deliberate treachery, and may have been a tactical mistake. However, it may also have been a practical response to the availability of shipping. It seems there were not enough vessels assembled at Dublin to convey Richard's whole force, so the bulk of the army had to march to Waterford in order to embark there.

Edward accompanied Richard to South Wales. They then advanced (very) slowly possibly because Edward's brother-in-law, Thomas Despenser, Earl of Gloucester, had been sent on to try to recruit men from his lordship of Glamorgan. Despenser failed in this attempt, and his return can only have damaged morale in the royal camp. It is likely that at around the same time Richard received word of York's capitulation to Bolingbroke outside Berkeley Castle.

Richard then inexplicably abandoned his army, and set off for North Wales with a small number of followers. Surprisingly, Edward was not among them. The most likely explanation is that the King believed there was a conspiracy against him, and that his cousin was part of it. York's surrender may have persuaded Richard that Edward had also turned against him. The Earl of Worcester, Northumberland's brother, was also left behind – Northumberland had joined Bolingbroke at Doncaster.

Edward and Worcester now found themselves in an unenviable position, deserted by the King and with the army dissolving around them in confusion. They evidently decided that there was nothing else for it but to cross Wales and submit to Henry. (In fairness, it is hard to see what else they *could* have done in the circumstances.)

Henry accepted his cousin's submission but rapidly stripped him (without any legal authority) of his offices of Lord High Constable of England and Constable of the Tower, and even of his recently-acquired manor of Burstwick. This tends to suggest that Edward had not been part of any prior conspiracy with Henry, although it would not be surprising if the two had kept in contact by letter during the latter's exile.

Edward was among those with Bolingbroke at Flint Castle for the meeting with the captured Richard II. Reportedly, Edward kept as far away from the King as possible. It is not known whether he kept equally far from his brother-in-law, who had accompanied Richard to the bitter end. To say the situation was awkward is putting it mildly.

Some accounts state that Edward and his father, York, visited King Richard in the Tower in an attempt to persuade him to abdicate. They were given short shrift, but Richard was eventually forced to abdicate. (Reports that he abdicated 'willingly' can be safely dismissed as Lancastrian propaganda.) He was also deposed by Parliament, although why this latter step was necessary if Richard had abdicated is not clear. In any event, Henry proceeded to claim the throne. Since he had complete military superiority at the time, it was impossible for anyone to object, even if they wished to do so.

Edward attended the coronation of Henry IV as Duke of Aumale, but shortly afterwards was arrested and imprisoned at Windsor Castle. He (along with other principal supporters of Richard II) was placed on trial before Parliament. While this must have been an uncomfortable experience for all of them, Edward became a particular target for attack, being accused, among other things, of the murder of the Duke of Gloucester. He was challenged to mortal combat by Lord Morley and Lord Fitzwalter – Philippa's stepson. Fortunately for him, the King intervened in proceedings. (It must be remembered that Henry himself had supported King Richard in 1397, and had actually given evidence against the Earl of Arundel. This seems to have been conveniently forgotten.)

Eventually, Edward was stripped of his Aumale title, and the lands granted to him since the 1397 Parliament. This was largely inevitable, given that the Earl of Warwick, and the heirs of Gloucester and Arundel, were to be restored. After a few weeks of more relaxed confinement, Edward was released and found himself on Henry's Council. In addition his right to the Isle of Wight was confirmed, as was his offices as Lieutenant of the Channel Islands and Justice in Eyre South of Trent.

John Holland, now reduced from Duke of Exeter to Earl of Huntingdon, and his nephew, Thomas Holland, now Earl of Kent instead of Duke of Surrey, were already plotting with the Earl of Salisbury and Thomas Despenser to overthrow the new King and restore Richard II. Rather surprisingly, they were joined in this plot by Lord Lumley, who was a life retainer of the Earl of Northumberland! According to the French chroniclers, Edward also entered into this plot, possibly with the intention of betraying it. English chroniclers are silent as to his involvement, and historians tend to downplay his participation.

If the French version is to be believed, Edward betrayed the plot (by accident or design) to his father, and the two of them then hurried to Windsor to warn Henry, who was literally hours from assassination. The King then managed to escape from Windsor and flee to London, where he was able to muster his forces. (The Londoners themselves were divided into pro and anti Richard factions, but there is little doubt the

Lancastrians were in the majority at this time, and Henry was safe among them.)

Whether Edward was responsible or not, it certainly seems that the King received last-minute warning from *someone*. The rebels, finding Henry gone, were thrown into confusion. They were a small force, and their main hope lay in killing Henry himself rather than meeting his supporters in a pitched battle. They retreated west in some disarray.

Edward was one of those who led Henry's forces against them. There was a battle of sorts at Maidenhead Bridge, but after that serious resistance crumbled, and an attack by local forces on the rebels at Cirencester effectively put paid to the rising. All the leading participants were butchered by the mobs that seized them, and many of their followers were subsequently executed, notably at Oxford.

If Edward did not betray his friends, he was unjustly treated by the French, who went to the trouble of hanging him in effigy outside the gates of Calais.

On 16 October 1400 Edward found himself made Governor of North Wales at the very time that Owain Glyndŵr's rising was in its initial stages. It is probable therefore that he was involved in the early counter-measures, which appeared, initially, to damp down the revolt. On 28 August 1401 he was appointed Lieutenant of Aquitaine, and left for Gascony. His stay there was short, but was also exceptionally expensive, causing debts which he claimed to amount to £10,000. This was much more than Edward - even as Duke of York - could hope to finance, and unfortunately it was also more than King Henry's over-stretched exchequer could supply. His father's death on 1 August 1402 may have made it necessary for him to return to England. He was home by November 1402.

He then petitioned for the wardship of his nephew, Richard Despenser, and custody of his lands. These were currently in the hands of his sister, Constance, Lady Despenser, and her patent had promised that they would not be removed from her, even if another person offered to pay more to the King for the privilege. This provision was swept aside and the wardship and with it a huge chunk of Despenser land came into Edward's possession on 17 May 1403. He was to hold on to this for the rest of his life.

His whereabouts at the time of the Battle of Shrewsbury (21 July 1403) are a complete mystery. All that can be said with certainty is he did not fight on either side. There were evidently some rumours as to his intentions, as the King felt obliged to declare that his cousin was loyal. Whatever Edward had or had not been up to in 1400, and again in 1403, there was clearly a body of opinion that believed him a traitor.

On 29 November 1403 he was made Keeper of Carmarthen Castle and Lieutenant of South Wales, Glyndŵr's activities having now spread to practically the whole of that country. Edward's financial difficulties were mounting all the time. Even the Despenser windfall was probably not as valuable as it might appear, given the hostilities in Wales. He had to borrow money from various sources, and was even forced to consider the sale of some of his lands. This latter was pretty much the ultimate humiliation for a nobleman of this era, and it is unlikely he was a contented subject given that Henry had buried him under so much debt.

He was, by his own eventual admission, at least *aware* of his sister's plot in February 1405 to remove the Mortimer boys from their confinement at Windsor Castle and take them to Glyndŵr. It is likely, in my opinion, that he was a lot more involved than that. The capture of Constance and the boys led to her examination before the Council, at which time she accused Edward of instigating the plot, and moreover of having sought to assassinate or at least imprison the King. Of course, by this time Constance had little cause to love her brother, who may have betrayed her husband and was certainly responsible for depriving her of her son and his lands. At first Edward denied everything, but was eventually forced to admit his knowledge of the conspiracy. He was probably lucky that there was no independent evidence against him, and he seems to have been given the benefit of the doubt.

Nevertheless, he was deprived of his lands and shut up in Pevensey Castle. Duchess Philippa was meanwhile confined to Fasterne in Wiltshire and made efforts on her husband's behalf. After a mere seventeen weeks in prison, York himself had the nerve to petition the King for release. He may have spent some of his jail time translating Gaston Phoebus' *Livre de la Chase* to which he added several chapters of his own. The completed work *The Master of Game* was dedicated to the Prince of Wales, and is available as a modern reprint. Edward served as Master of Hart Hounds to Henry IV, in which role he was possibly more reliable than in some of his more political offices.

On 7 October he was summoned to the King, who was at this time at Worcester. Shortly afterwards Henry IV moved to Kenilworth, where Constance was confined. This may not have been a coincidence. Having overcome his enemies in 1405 – despite having a Franco-Welsh army camped outside Worcester for a time – Henry was perhaps in a mood to begin to forgive his cousins. Before 26 November Edward was set free, and his lands were restored to him in December. Within a few months he was opening Parliament on behalf of the sickly King! On 1 November 1406 he was once again appointed Constable of the Tower.

Edward now assisted the Prince of Wales in the continuing campaign against Glyndŵr. In September 1407 he was involved in the siege of Aberystwyth Castle, and evidently played an important part. The Prince reported to Parliament that the Duke of York *had served and laboured in such a way as to support and embolden all the other members of the company, as if he had been the poorest gentleman in the realm wishing to serve him in order to win honour and renown.*

On 16 May 1409 Edward, in common with several other individuals, was ordered to live continually on his Welsh lands. Since he had none of his own, this would have meant in practice those Despenser lands in Wales for which he was responsible.

On 18th December 1411 Edward was licensed to found Fotheringhay College. This involved placing a large proportion of his lands into the hands of feoffees to ensure the work could be financed. He was responsible for a new Chancel for the church and the associated collegiate buildings. These were not completed until after his death, and, sadly, they were all destroyed in the 16th Century. The surviving part of the church – built in the same style – is the new Nave erected by his nephew and successor.

In 1412 Edward accompanied the Duke of Clarence (Henry IV's second son) on an expedition to Gascony in support of the Armagnac faction. The two parties in France came to a settlement before the English became engaged in the war, but heavy compensation was nevertheless extracted to cover the costs of the intrusion. Edward was still in Aquitaine in June 1413 – during his stay there he had attempted to interest the

King of Aragon in supporting his claim to the throne of Castile. Even if Edward had a clique of supporters in Spain, it is highly unlikely that he could have afforded to pursue this crown. Moreover, given the political situation, it is even more unlikely that the new king, Henry V, would have allowed him to divert English military resources in this way. Nevertheless, the House of York never forgot its claim to Castile, and Edward IV was later to display its heraldry along with his own.

By 31 August 1414 Edward was in Paris, attempting to arrange the marriage of Henry V to Katherine of Valois. This was to be his last diplomatic mission and, it may be observed, his second attempt to marry a king of England to one of Charles VI's daughters. On this occasion he was unsuccessful.

Edward was a trusted adviser of Henry V, being appointed Justiciar of South Wales in July 1414, and Keeper of Berwick and Warden of the East March in September of the same year. Following the death of his nephew, Richard Despenser, he even managed to keep control of the Despenser estates that were in his hands, though they should have passed to his niece, Isabelle Despenser, and her husband Richard Beauchamp Lord Bergavenny.

He accompanied Henry V to France in the military expedition to France, and made his will during the siege of Harfleur, describing himself as *of all sinners the most wretched and guilty* and taking care to leave Philippa a generous share of his goods. He was killed at the Battle of Agincourt, on 25th October 1415, while leading the English vanward. It is generally stated he was crushed to death in the throng, and as one of the leading English nobles present he would have been a magnet for French enemies trying to gain a ransom. It is also claimed that it was Edward who suggested that the English archers should be protected by sharpened stakes. Given his experience this seems quite plausible.

His remains were brought back to Fotheringhay and buried under a brass in the Chancel. This part of the church having fallen into ruin during her brother's reign, Queen Elizabeth I had Edward's bones moved to a new monument, which still survives in Fotheringhay Church.

Edward had no children by his wife and - although it is known he was involved with at least one mistress - nor is there any reference to his having children by anyone else. Philippa survived him by many years, despite being his senior, and was eventually buried in Westminster Abbey following her death in 1431. Ironically, she has the finest tomb of any of the York family of her generation.

The Chronicler of Godstow considered Edward a *second Solomon*. Though he knew when to change sides, and occasionally made a fool of himself, it is clear that the second Duke of York was far from the amiable buffoon so many authors of fiction have made him.

DAUGHTER OF YORK

Constance of York, Lady Le Despenser and Countess of Gloucester

In view of the known birth date of her elder brother it's unlikely that Constance was born before 1374 but she must have been around before 7 November 1379, when an entry in John of Gaunt's Register records a gift for her (earlier) marriage to Thomas le Despenser. As with her brother, Edward, we have no knowledge of her place of birth.

The gift in question was a silver-gilt cup and ewer on a stand, costing £22-0s-4d. Constance was a relatively rare name in England at this time and it seems likely (though I cannot prove it) that Constance, Duchess of Lancaster, her aunt twice over, was also her godmother.

In April 1378, Edmund of Langley had been granted the marriage of Thomas Despenser's elder brother, Edward, for the benefit of his daughter. However the young heir died in the interim and Thomas was substituted. (This was a case where wardship and marriage were kept separate, as the *wardship* remained with Thomas's mother.) Thomas, born 1373, was just a few years older than his wife who cannot have been above five, *at most*, at the time of the ceremony. I believe she may have been younger still.

Thomas was the great-grandson of the famous (or infamous) Hugh Despenser the Younger, close friend, minister and possibly lover of King Edward II. Hugh's fall from power had been a complete disaster for the Despenser family, but Thomas' grandfather, great-uncle and father had successively rebuilt their reputation, and to a very large extent their fortune. Thomas' father, Edward Despenser, was a famous and highly-respected knight, associated with the Black Prince (and to a lesser extent with John of Gaunt, Duke of Lancaster) who had achieved a fair degree of martial glory in France, as well as marrying Elizabeth de Burghersh, a substantial heiress and baroness in her own right. The family estates included lands in numerous English counties, with a strong concentration in Gloucestershire and Worcestershire, and the Marcher Lordship of Glamorgan, the richest and juiciest plum in a whole basket of such plums. Although ranked as a mere baron, Despenser was (on reaching his majority) among the top dozen or so richest laymen in England and (as far as actual income from land was concerned) somewhat richer than his father-in-law.

(It would be astonishing if the Lordship of Glamorgan, prior to the damaging Welsh rising of the early fifteenth century, did not produce at least the £1,500 a year that Henry Bolingbroke is known to have received from his lordship of Brecon. £2,000 or north thereof is more likely. A proportion of this would go to Thomas' mother as her dower, but of course there were also substantial English estates. Even on the lower estimate, Thomas' share of the Glamorgan revenue alone would more than equal Edmund of Langley's entire income from land.)

During Thomas' minority Edmund of Langley was granted various annuities funded by the Despenser estates including, in January 1384, 80 marks per annum towards Constance's maintenance. I have calculated (from various figures given in T.B. Pugh's *Henry V and the Southampton Plot*) that York's personal income *from lands* was less than £1000 a year at best, which means he was not even in the same league as his brother Lancaster. (If we think of Gaunt as the Manchester City of Richard II's court, then Langley was perhaps Rotherham United.) Therefore, any additions were no doubt gratefully received.

In 1386 Constance was made a Dame of the Garter, not quite its youngest-ever member but not far off. This honour was in her own right, though quite possibly intended to please her father, who was created Duke of York in 1385. It is worth noting that Richard II appointed more women to the Garter than all the other medieval kings put together. If one bears in mind the later complaint that he had 'too many ladies' at his Court, it suggests that, whatever faults he may have had, he had a liking for female company.

She had at least three children by Despenser and, unusually the dates of birth are known for two of them. These were

Richard (b 30 November 1396), Elizabeth, and Isabelle (born – posthumously – 26 July 1400.) Some sources add other children, but these are the only ones mentioned in the *Tewkesbury Chronicle.* Hugh Despenser, who died 1401, is sometimes referenced – but as he was leading armies before Thomas and Constance were of an age to produce children, it seems more likely that the Hugh in question was Thomas' cousin of that name.

Although he spent some time in the household of and was knighted in the field by Richard II's enemy, Richard Fitzalan, Earl of Arundel, Thomas Despenser eventually became a partisan of the King. (His mother Elizabeth received exoneration for all responsibility concerning his custody until he returned from Arundel's military expedition.)

On 20 May 1391 Thomas received a royal licence to travel to Prussia with a retinue of 50 persons to take part in one the fashionable 'crusades' against the Lithuanians. Or so it used to be believed. Recent research suggests that the 'Lord Despenser' in question was his cousin, Hugh. Which is slightly odd, as Hugh was never a peer. This leaves us with a gap in Thomas' career. All that can be said is that his marriage to Constance probably drew him closer, politically and personally, to the House of York and King Richard.

In 1394 he accompanied the King on his Irish expedition, and just prior to this, on 7th March, was given full livery of his lands, though still a few months short of 21. He was however required to pay a rent, which was terminated on 10 September.

Despenser was one of those (along with Constance's brother, Edward) who 'appealed' the earls of Warwick and Arundel and the Duke of Gloucester of treason in the Parliament of 1397. His reward was to be created Earl of Gloucester and be given a share of the confiscated lands. Unusually these were granted to him and Constance in jointure, which suggests particular regard for Constance's interests either on his part or that of her cousin, Richard II. Unfortunately for her, they were taken away by Henry IV's first Parliament, and there is nothing to suggest she had any other land in jointure.

Two pardons are recorded for persons accused of murder on 22 June 1395 and April 27 1396 'at the request of our beloved kinswoman the Countess of Gloucester.' Constance did not of course become Countess until 1397, so it's likely these were actually procured by her aunt, Eleanor, Duchess of Gloucester. However it does seem a very odd slip for a clerk's pen to make.

Thomas Despenser seems to have been less favoured after 1397 and received no further rewards, but nevertheless he remained loyal to Richard II and was one of the handful of men captured with the King at Conwy. After the accession of Henry IV, Constance and her husband attended the new sovereign's coronation. Shortly after this, Thomas was arrested and placed in the Tower where, to judge from the birth date of his last child, Constance joined him.

Following a trial in Parliament by which he was reduced in rank to Lord Despenser of Glamorgan and Morganwg and stripped of the lands gained in 1397, Thomas was released and before long appointed to Henry's Council. There is evidence he considered going on crusade, either to Prussia or Rhodes, and had he done so he might have prolonged his life. As it was he joined the disastrous Epiphany Plot against Bolingbroke. After its failure he was captured and killed at Bristol, without any legal process. His head was sent for by the King and placed on London Bridge, but his mother arranged for it to be recovered and almost certainly made provision for his burial by the monks of Tewkesbury.

(The evidence he was involved in the plot is in fact strangely limited, but his flight from Cardiff and death at the hands of the Bristolians is suggestive, as is his subsequent attainder. Some accounts don't even mention his participation.)

Constance's location during these dramatic events is unknown, but her husband's death in such circumstances deprived her of everything she possessed, and certainly any claim to dower rights. She sent in a succession of petitions to Henry IV and eventually secured a share of Despenser's goods, her son's wardship and the possession of most of the Despenser lands. It appears she also held by way of lease at least part of her mother-in-law's dower lands, although how this came about is not clear.

In fairness to Henry IV it must be stated that she was treated far better than any of the other widows – apart from the King's own sister, Elizabeth, Duchess of Exeter. This may be because of the respect (and political debt) Henry owed to her father, or simply recognition of her closeness in blood. The Countess of Wiltshire, whose husband had been summarily executed by Henry prior to his accession in an act of sheer terrorism, was by contrast reduced to abject poverty. Nevertheless, Constance was left in the position of a tenant-at-will – her husband's formal attainder by the Parliament of 1401 only served to spell this out, and she was careful to secure a fresh grant of confirmation from the King, as a means of being as sure as possible.

Thomas Despenser had had a house close to the Minoresses Convent near Tower Hill. A door had been made so he could enter their church from his house. In 1402 the nuns petitioned the Pope that the door be blocked as the house had fallen to a 'temporal lady' who was presuming to make use of the entrance. It seems at least possible that this 'temporal lady', carefully unnamed, was none other than Constance of York – though it is slightly odd that the nuns should object to a woman entering their church when they had apparently been happy for Thomas to do so! Perhaps they found her rather more abrasive than her late husband. Her cousin, Isabel of Gloucester, was a member of the Community of the Minories. She had no cause to love Constance given the involvement of the latter's husband and brother in the downfall and death of her father, Thomas of Woodstock, Duke of Gloucester. Indeed, there had even been rumours that Thomas had poisoned Isabel's brother, Humphrey. (It is hard to see how Despenser could have done, given that he and Humphrey were separated by the Irish Sea at the time of the boy's death. Nevertheless, grief is not always completely rational.)

In January, 1403 the first clear sign of tension between Constance and the King is recorded when she was ordered to release (or bring before him) certain tenants of his lordship of Ogmore whom she had in her jail at Cardiff. This order apparently had to be repeated several times before she obeyed it; if indeed she obeyed it at all. The tenants in question were all Welshmen, but how they had offended is not recorded.

A few weeks later, coincidentally or not, her son's wardship was taken from her (despite written assurance in her patent that it would not be) and given to her brother, the Duke of York. This was undoubtedly related to the impressive debt Henry owned York for services in Gascony, but one doubts whether Constance was happy that the King should pay his debts to her brother at her expense, quite apart from the issue of her losing control of her son, who was still some months short of seven years old.

Later on in the year she was ordered to secure her castles at Caerphilly and Ewyas Lacy (Longtown) against the Welsh rebels, but it's unlikely she had the funds to do this adequately. (These castles were technically held in dower by Elizabeth Despenser, but as mentioned above it appears that at some point Elizabeth had farmed them out to her daughter-in-law – or possibly to her son before his death.)

The Welsh rebellion was of course the one led by Owain Glyndŵr, and although initially confined to the north, by 1403 it was very seriously impacting on Constance's lands in Glamorgan. Her income would certainly have been severely hit. Indeed, as far as her Welsh lands were concerned, it's probable there was no net income at all for some years.

The Parliament of 1404 granted Constance's petition that she should be allowed her dower rights – which were usually denied to the widow of an attainted traitor. This gave a much more satisfactory title to the lands she already held, but obtaining her full dower rights was less straightforward, particularly during the life of her brother, Edward, who was sitting on the bulk of the Despenser properties by the right of his recently-obtained wardship of her son. It is not clear whether she ever succeeded in obtaining her dower lands in full.

Around this time Constance began a *liaison* with Edmund Holland, Earl of Kent, who was some years her junior. He was the son of Richard II's elder half-brother, Thomas Holland and his wife, Alice Arundel (or Fitzalan), sister of the Arundel executed in 1397. His elder brother, Thomas, Duke of Surrey, had been high in King Richard's favour and – like Thomas Despenser - had died in the Epiphany rising of early 1400. Kent himself had been arrested with his sister-in-law at Liverpool after landing there from Ireland soon after Surrey's death. However, he was soon released – his influential relatives included his uncle, Thomas Arundel, Archbishop of Canterbury – and restored to a portion of the Holland estates, albeit under Henry's wardship. In a short career Kent was to prove both a warrior – beginning by fighting on Henry's side at the Battle of Shrewsbury (1403) – and a formidable jouster.

He was Constance's uncle by marriage as his sister, Joan, or Joanne had married Constance's father *circa* 1393. Their association probably began at court as one chronicler indirectly mentions her as being in the household of Queen Joanna of Navarre, who married Henry IV in 1402.

The only evidence of this connection is that a daughter, Alianore, was born. Alianore later married Lord Audley and claimed to be legitimate. There may indeed have been some sort of secret marriage ceremony *a la mode* Edward IV, but although Alianore had enough evidence to take to a spiritual court, Kent's other heirs – headed by the Duchess of Clarence - had the matter quashed by the Parliament of 1431. It is interesting to note that the decision of Parliament was given force even in the event of the bishop's court deciding in the Audleys' favour. The much-vaunted power of the spiritual courts over matters of marriage clearly had little practical effect once Parliament was involved.

(It is of interest that the heirs claimed that Constance had been present at the public marriage between Kent and Lucia of Milan in 1407. *If this was true*, and if Constance had not protested at the time, it would certainly have invalidated any irregular marriage between her and Kent. However, if it really was the case, the heirs should have been confident of victory in the spiritual court, and ought not to have needed to involve Parliament.)

In early 1405 Kent even went as far as to obtain a licence to marry 'whom he would of the King's allegiance' but the ink was scarcely dry on this grant before Constance removed the Mortimer boys from Windsor Castle in the night and headed for Wales.

These Mortimers were the sons of Roger Mortimer, Earl of March (d. 1398) and were regarded by many as right heirs to the throne. (They were also Kent's nephews.) They were under a sort of house arrest, sometimes at Windsor, sometimes at Berkhampstead. Although kept under lock and key – certainly at night – they were probably not much worse off than other children of their rank living in a stranger's household.

Constance's intention was obviously to take them to Glyndŵr and the boys' uncle, Sir Edmund Mortimer, who had defected to Glyndŵr after the Battle of Pilleth (1402). Glyndŵr and Mortimer would certainly have used them as figureheads in a grand revolt. As it was her party was overtaken nearly Cheltenham (perilously close to the Severn and probable safety) and although the grand revolt of 1405 *did* take place it was badly co-ordinated and defeated in detail, albeit with some tricky moments for King Henry. (An example of the difficulty of analysing the events of 1405 is that accounts differ as to whether the famous stand-off near Worcester between Henry and a Franco-Welsh force took place in 1404 or 1405, or whether it took place at all. Henry was at Worcester at the relevant time in 1405 but not in 1404.)

What exactly Constance was doing at Windsor is not clear. She was certainly there at Christmas 1404, as she received a grant of wine from the King, but the court was at Eltham. Some accounts say she was acting as the boys' governess. This may seem unlikely, but if we reject it we have to find some other reason for her being on 'detached duty' at Windsor. In any event she obviously secured access to the boys and was able to arrange their escape from one of the country's major strongholds. This must have involved time and careful planning, and the less 'official' contact she had, the harder it would be.

The boys were returned to custody and the elder, Edmund, was released in Henry V's reign and enjoyed his inheritance as

Earl of March, albeit he was always under the suspicion of the authorities until he died. The younger boy, Roger, died while still in custody. Their sister, Anne, secretly married Constance's brother, Richard of Conisbrough, later Earl of Cambridge, at some point before 1408. They were of course the parents of Richard, 3rd Duke of York and grandparents of Edward IV and Richard III.

When Constance was brought before the Council to explain herself she threw the blame on her brother York, and when he denied it offered trial by combat – with a champion fighting for herself of course. A champion, Richard Maidstone, duly stepped forward, but the King, possibly with memories of the fiasco at Gosford Green in 1397 in mind, refused to allow the combat. (Had it ended in victory for York, Constance would have been burnt at the stake, so she had chosen a high-risk strategy.) If Constance had expected Kent to offer to fight for her to she was severely disappointed.

No formal trial ensued, but Constance was stripped of lands and goods and imprisoned at Kenilworth Castle. Despite much verbal wriggling York – who had repeatedly been accused of treason during Henry's reign – was treated similarly, and locked up at Pevensey Castle. The only person to suffer capital punishment was the locksmith who had made false keys for Constance. (Rank undoubtedly had its advantages.)

As referred to above, it seems highly likely that the York brother and sister were up to their neck in a more general plot including Glyndŵr, Edmund Mortimer, Northumberland, Archbishop Scrope and the Earl Marshal, all of whom had shown their hand or were about to. There must be a fair chance that Kent was involved as well, but he retained Henry's favour and was not to join the rebellion that broke out later in the year.

By late autumn York was released and before much longer was opening Parliament on behalf of his sickly cousin! (He soon obtained effective control of the Despenser estates and, apart from Constance's portion, held on to most of them until his death.) Constance was also eventually released, though it is by no means clear exactly when this happened. She received an order for the restoration of 'all the goods that belonged to the said Constance, in the custody of the Treasurer of our Household,' (19 January 1406) just over £56 for 'expenses', (March 1406) and then her lands, (June 18 1406) her petitioning skills coming to the fore once again.

It is not clear whether she did attend Kent's wedding – as his heirs alleged she did – or what pressure Henry IV placed on her in this matter, if any. Kent is usually said to have married Lucia of Milan at Southwark on 24 January 1407. (Wylie states some months later.) Constance was in any case not in a strong position to object to Kent's marriage, which had been arranged by King Henry himself, a marriage contract having been signed in May 1406, while she was quite possibly still locked away in Kenilworth and certainly still in the process of regaining her landed endowment from forfeiture. Indeed, nor was Kent given the free choice of bride he had been promised. His consent to the marriage may have been bought by Lucia's notional dowry of 70,000 florins, which would have been good news for Kent, and even better for his many creditors, had it actually been paid. Unfortunately it was not, and when he was killed by a crossbow bolt to his head in September 1408 during a raid on Brittany, he left debts behind him of over 4,000 marks. Constance was fortunate that it was Lucia, rather than she, who had to deal with the consequences.

(As an aside, it is not clear why Henry IV went to the trouble of importing Lucia of Milan as a bride for Kent. It is unlikely that the marriage was of any diplomatic benefit, as Kent was not an immediate member of Henry's family, only a fairly remote cousin. As for Lucia herself, she was one of many daughters of Bernarbo Visconti, Lord of Milan, who had been deposed and murdered as long ago as 1385. While her exact age is not known, it is unlikely she was significantly younger than Constance. She had met Bolingbroke during his visit to Milan in the 1390s and had gone so far as to declare that she would marry no one else. Her cousin, Gian Galeazzo (who had succeeded her father after deposing him) had been on excellent terms with Henry, and at one point had actually suggested Lucia as a bride for him. Needless to say, this had not come to fruition, and Gian Galeazzo had died in 1402. That the Milanese should have offered such a huge dowry for Lucia – had it materialised it would have been the largest paid in

England in the whole fifteenth century — is frankly inexplicable.)

In May 1409, Constance was among a number of landowners ordered to live on their Welsh estates (or what remained of them after the recent devastation) as a precautionary measure against Glyndŵr's rebels, although the greatest danger to English rule was over by this time.

After that she lived fairly quietly, only the occasional legal dispute troubling the records, notably one in 1409 when she attempted to claim a free man as her serf — a favourite trick of the nobility when struggling for ready cash. Having imprisoned the man and prevented his recovery by the County Sheriff, she was brought before the King's Bench Court on a writ of *capias* and claimed that as a peer of the realm *capias* did not lie against her and further alleged her opponent was her villein. The Court allowed the man to find surety to sue his case that he was free.

In 1410 she claimed two men, Robert Stokes and John Abraham to be her serfs. The Sheriff was ordered by the King to free the men but was not allowed to see them. The men were however later delivered to the Court by her servants, Robert Rous and Hugh Holgot, the judges having been ordered by the King to try the case. Whether this was a repeat of the case taken to the King's Bench in 1409, a legitimate case of serfs who had left her lands without leave or a fresh attempt to extort cash is not clear.

The Close Rolls contain an order of Henry V dated 18 February 1415 to the escheators of various counties that Constance was to have her dower, not withstanding any previous grants to the contrary or forfeitures of treason. On December 8 of the same year, her son-in-law, Richard Beauchamp, Lord Bergavenny (later Earl of Worcester) was specifically ordered to hand over to Constance a long list of lands in South Wales, Gloucestershire and the Marches. It is likely that Beauchamp had only recently clawed these lands out of the maw of the House of York (in the person of Duke Edward) and was now required to hand them over to Constance.

Two of Constance's children predeceased her, as did her two brothers – Richard, Earl of Cambridge was executed in 1415 and York died at Agincourt later the same year. Henry V had confirmed his father's grants to her on 18 July 1413.

Constance herself died on 28 November 1416. Writs of *diem clausit extremum* were issued the same day, which implies that she died somewhere within easy reach of Westminster. Be that as it may, she was buried before the high altar of Reading Abbey. (Though the abbey is now a total ruin, she is somewhere near King Henry I whose grave is marked.) As she owned a very attractive manor and park just across the Thames at Caversham, she may well have become a patron of the Abbey. It was extremely unusual for any member of the Despenser family *not* to be buried in Tewkesbury Abbey, but Constance was anything but a conformist. In 1448 her little great-granddaughter, Anne Beauchamp, child heiress of Henry, Duke of Warwick, was laid to rest in the same tomb. She should therefore be easy to identify if some future archaeologist is permitted to investigate the site.

Constance's eldest daughter, Elizabeth, was still alive in 1404, when she and her sister Isabelle were in the care of one of the King's yeomen, but she did not grow to adulthood and is said to be buried in St. Mary's Church, Cardiff.

Constance's son Richard died around 1413. He had been married to Alianore (or Eleanor) Neville, eldest daughter of Ralph, Earl of Westmorland and his second wife, Joan Beaufort, who was of course one of Constance's many first cousins. Alianore was subsequently married to Henry Percy, Earl of Northumberland, and after many years of striving, eventually managed to secure her Despenser dower of £500 a year.

Constance's second Despenser daughter Isabelle married two cousins, each called Richard Beauchamp. The second and more famous one was the Earl of Warwick, and from this marriage descended Queen Anne Neville, Isabelle, Duchess of Clarence and the Blessed Margaret Pole, as well as, eventually, Diana, Princess of Wales and many others. Isabelle's splendid chantry chapel may still be found in Tewkesbury Abbey (where she is buried with her first husband and just a few feet away from her father, son, brother and grandparents.) Careful inspection of the chantry will reveal a shield bearing Constance's arms, though it is rather faded. A lock of Isabelle's hair (golden blonde) is preserved in Tewkesbury Museum.

Constance's descendants through Alianore, Lady Audley are positively legion and are said to include Robert. E. Lee, the Confederate general, and Humphrey Bogart.

RICHARD THE OBSCURE

Richard of Conisbrough, Earl of Cambridge

Many historians take the view that Richard of Conisbrough was born around 1375. There is no evidence to support this, and some suggestive evidence he was not. In passing, I ought to mention that in his lifetime he was usually known as Lord Richard of York. Historians tend to refer to him by his birthplace, Conisbrough, as a means of distinguishing him from his much more famous son, Richard the 3rd Duke of York.

T.B. Pugh in *Henry V and the Southampton Plot* postulates that Richard was born in 1385. While no direct evidence can be produced to support this theory, such a date of birth fits well with the few known facts of Richard's life. Pugh also suggests that Richard may have been the son, not of Edmund of Langley, but of John Holland, Earl of Huntingdon and (later) Duke of Exeter, the younger of King Richard II's Holland half-brothers. This theory is based on the belief held by some Chaucerian Scholars that Chaucer's poem *The Complaint of Mars* relates to an affair between Holland and Duchess Isabella. This 'tradition' is based up a note by Shirley, a fifteenth century bibliophile, who, interestingly enough, had known connections with Isabella's granddaughters, Isabelle Despenser, Countess of Warwick and Isabel of Cambridge, Countess of Essex. He may, or may not, have been told the tale by one of these ladies. In 1385 Edmund of Langley was certainly in Yorkshire, as part of the great army Richard II assembled to invade Scotland. He might have taken his wife as far as his castle of Conisbrough. However, it cannot be stressed too much that this is conjecture, not fact. We simply do not know when Richard was born, still less is there any proof that his father was anyone other than Edmund of Langley.

What we do know is that in his will Edmund of Langley left Richard precisely nothing. By this time it was normal practice for a younger son of the high nobility to be provided with at least some land. Usually this was purchased, to avoid touching the eldest's sons patrimony, and it's possible that York was simply too poor to acquire a manor or two for this purpose. On the other hand, it is somewhat odd that Richard was not at least left some token bequest – a sword for example, or a ring. He was not.

In her will, Duchess Isabella left all her jewels (her most valuable asset) to Richard II, with a request that he provide for her younger son. In return the King granted his cousin (and godson) an annuity of £223-6-8 at the Exchequer. It was not, however, paid until March 1395, over two years after Isabella's death. The delay in itself suggests that Richard was not a grown man at the time of his mother's death.

It need hardly be said that grants at the Exchequer were all well and good while the Exchequer had money in it, but not as desirable as a grant of land, from which a secure income could normally be expected. However Richard was at the back of a very long queue, which included his own father and elder brother, for the limited amount of land that became available over the years, and in fact he never received any in his own right.

Another possible indication of Richard's youth is the fact he was neither knighted, given an office, nor granted a title during Richard II's reign, despite the high favour in which his family stood. Indeed his first recorded public appearance was in the coronation procession of Henry IV, in which he took precedence over the barons of England. Rather surprisingly, given that he was the King's cousin and that his father had assisted Henry's accession, he was not knighted on this occasion either.

Where Richard lived after his father's death in 1402 is not clear. Given the chaotic state of Henry IV's finances, especially in the early years it is unlikely that he was able to secure his annuity in full, if at all, for some time. This would have put him in great financial difficulty, and probably unable to maintain a household of his own. He may have had no choice but to live in his brother's household, or, just possibly, his sister's. Either way, we do not catch sight of him again until 1403, when he was apparently leading a small armed force in Herefordshire. He was in the highly embarrassing position of not being able to pay his soldiers. For how long he took part in the struggle against Glyndŵr is not known, but clearly risking his life in the adventure failed to make him a rich man. If, like Edward, he took part in Henry, Prince of Wales' later campaigns against Owain, his presence has not been recorded.

At some point before 1408, he married Anne Mortimer, daughter of Roger Mortimer, Earl of March (killed 1398) and sister to the present young and imprisoned March. All that can be said for certain is that the marriage was irregular and secret. It *may* have been arranged for political reasons by Richard's ambitious brother and sister who, as we have seen, were in 1404/1405 involved in intrigues to bring down Henry IV and replace him with March. On the other hand, Pugh points out that during his service in the Marches, Richard probably established a working relationship with Anne's stepfather, Edward Charleton, Lord of Powys. It is even possible it was a love match. Certainly, it was not a marriage made with immediate financial gain in mind. Anne was even poorer than Richard, sharing an annuity of £100 with her sister Eleanor and probably not receiving much of it.

It is of some interest that one of the defects in the marriage dispensed by the Pope was a lack of parental consent. However, the last surviving blood parent, Alianore, Countess of March, died in 1405. The reference *may* be to Anne's stepfather, Lord Charleton, but it is impossible to be sure. Richard would have come of age (if Pugh's assumptions are correct) in 1406, while Anne, who as a woman only needed to be 14, achieved that status in 1404. (These are the ages for inheritance free from wardship; the age of consent to marriage was 14 for males and 12 for females.)

In 1406, Richard was chosen as a member of the escort sent with King Henry's daughter, Philippa, to her wedding in Denmark. Pugh suggests a reason for his selection was that he was 'the least important (and most expendable) member of the English royal house.' This is a harsh, but probably fair assessment of Richard's status in the world. Nevertheless, he was knighted in July 1406 to mark the occasion, and also paid his expenses in advance, which must have made him feel, temporarily, as rich as Croesus, given that the figure was almost a hundred pounds more than his normal (and at this time somewhat theoretical) annual allowance from the Exchequer.

In May, 1408 Richard and Anne received a Papal Dispensation regularising their marriage. This was an example that their grandson, Edward IV might have profited from. In the following year, following the death of Anne's uncle, the Earl of Kent, the couple received their very first piece of landed estate, a share of her late mother's portion of the Holland inheritance. (It should be noted that this is the route by which certain Holland lands came to be attached to the duchy of York. It had nothing to do, as is sometimes suggested, with Edmund of Langley's marriage to Joanne Holland. Although when Joanne herself died in 1434, *her* share was partitioned between the heirs of her sisters, including Richard, Duke of York.)

Richard and Anne had at least two children; Isabel, later Countess of Essex, born 1408, and Richard, later third Duke of York, born 1411. There may have been another son, Henry, who died young.

Soon after the birth of her son, Richard, Anne Mortimer died. She was buried at King's Langley in the same tomb as her parents-in-law, but no details of the funeral have survived. Given her husband's stretched financial circumstances, it was almost certainly a low-key affair.

At some unknown time Edward, Duke of York appointed his brother as deputy in his office as Warden of the Channel Islands. He was acting in this role in both 1409 and 1412, but when the appointment took effect, and whether Richard spent time in the Channel Islands is not known. (It is possible the appointment was purely a sinecure.) Richard also appears to have acquired the right to live at Conisbrough Castle, which belonged to Edward, but no formal lease or other form of grant has come down to us. Apart from this there is nothing to show that Richard acted as one of his brother's officers or was given any responsibility by York.

Round about 1414, Richard married Maud Clifford, who was the daughter of Thomas, Lord Clifford and his wife Elizabeth Roos. She was also the 'divorced' wife of John Neville, Lord

Latimer, that marriage having been annulled on the grounds that Latimer had failed to consummate it. Certain of Latimer's lands had been conveyed to feoffees (roughly equivalent to trustees in the modern sense) as a jointure for Maud. Rather surprisingly, the feoffees declined to give Latimer his property back, and Maud was able to retain them for the term of her life. This property of his new wife's elevated Richard to something approaching modest prosperity, certainly when compared to the thin years of Henry IV's early reign. However, he was still very far from wealthy, considering his status as a member of the King's family.

Some sources claim a child of this marriage, Alice, who later married Thomas Musgrave. The evidence for this daughter's existence is somewhat mixed, and requires further confirmation.

On 1 May 1414, Richard was created Earl of Cambridge in Parliament. This had been one of his brother's subsidiary titles, which Edward had (presumably) resigned so that his heir-presumptive could enjoy it. Unusually, no endowment of any kind was granted with the earldom, not even the proverbial pie's nest. So, although Richard was now an earl, he was by a very long way the poorest of the breed, and did not have anything like the livelihood necessary to support the honour. He did not possess a single foot of land in his own right, although Henry V did retain him with a sum of 500 marks a year. He was the very first landless earl in English history.

Whether this lack of endowment preyed on Richard's mind, we cannot know. However, he now became the centre of a plot to destroy Henry V. A foolish and ill-conceived plot, it must be said. There is nothing to show that his siblings were involved, but he undoubtedly used his other family connections.

Sir Thomas Gray of Heton had a son, also Thomas, who in 1412 was 'married' to Richard's daughter, Isabel, who was certainly no more than four years old at the time. The other connection was that Gray had bought the lordship of Tyndale from the Duke of York, with a view to it being settled on Isabel and her husband. Although Tyndale was sold at a bargain price of £500 (no doubt because of Edward's own lack of ready cash) Gray struggled to pay the instalments and most of the price was still outstanding when he was executed. Sir Thomas was one of the many sons-in-law of Ralph Neville, Earl of Westmorland, and his family was of importance among the Border gentry. However, he was far from being a magnate.

If Gray and Cambridge had threadbare purses, this cannot be said of the third of the main plotters, Henry, Lord Scrope of Masham. Scrope's connection with Cambridge was that he was the latest husband of the latter's stepmother, Joanne Holland, Duchess of York. Scrope had bargained with Joanne that she could choose £2,000 worth of his goods in return for agreeing to relinquish any claim she might have (as his future widow) to one third or one half of his movables. It does not take much imagination to see that his movable goods must have added up to substantially more than this. His income and Joanne's taken together was in the region of £1,800 a year – by the standards of northern barons a very tidy sum indeed. Such wealth dwarfed Cambridge's meagre incomings.

Scrope had been on reasonably good terms with Henry V, and his reasons for joining the plot are not obvious. He was to claim that his intention was to betray it. This may be true, but if so he miscalculated badly.

Cambridge sought to bring his brother-in-law, Lord Clifford into the plot, but Clifford was too wise to have anything to do with it.

The plot itself had several strands, most of them feeble. One was to bring the person posing as Richard II in Scotland into England in exchange for a suitable hostage. By 1415 it is unlikely there were many people around who still thought Richard II was alive, although it is interesting that there were some. Another aspect was to arrange a similar exchange for Henry Percy (son of Hotspur who had been killed fighting Henry IV at Shrewsbury in 1403.) Henry Percy was (once his father and grandfather's attainder were reversed) Earl of Northumberland and it must be admitted that the Percy family had many partisans in the North. However, Percy had already come to terms with Henry V for his return from exile and at least partial reinstatement, and it is unlikely that Cambridge's offer was anything near as attractive.

Murdoch, Earl of Fife, a Scottish hostage, was seized by Henry Talbot (a Yorkshire squire who may have been working with Cambridge) but Fife's prompt recapture put paid to any prospect of a swap for either 'Richard II' or Percy. It seems unlikely that such an exchange would have helped matters anyway, while Richard's hopes for further support in the North seem to have been wishful thinking.

The next strand was to involve the Earl of March and the Welsh. Edmund Mortimer, Earl of March, had been kept prisoner by the Lancastrians for many years, and following his release had been made to pay a ridiculous amount of money to marry his chosen bride. So he did have reason to oppose Henry V, and in theory had a lot of tenants who could have been mobilised. As for the Welsh, the Glyndŵr rising was in theory still smouldering, but at a very low ebb. Owain himself may have been dead by this time – no one is quite sure. In any event, Cambridge was only able to obtain the support of David Howell from Pembrokeshire, a squire of no particular importance. It is doubtful whether Richard had any significant contacts in Wales, and if he did he certainly failed to gain their support.

March seems to have thought the matter over – and then betrayed the conspiracy to Henry V. While it is easy to criticise him – he seems to have been a notably ineffectual individual – in this matter at least he was a good judge. The plot was far too weak and insufficiently developed to have had a hope of success. It is even questionable whether it was – technically – high treason. The indictments against Cambridge, Scrope and Gray claimed that they intended to kill the King and his brothers, but it is not clear they had got much beyond rather dubious scheming. Scrope in particular may have been guilty of misprision at worst. In any event, all three confessed, although sadly the confessions are mutilated and incomplete. Naturally they all sought to minimise their own guilt.

Gray was tried before a Hampshire jury, Cambridge and Scope by a panel of their peers. All were inevitably found guilty and beheaded.

Parliament later confirmed the validity of the sentences, although Richard, Earl of Cambridge was not formally attainted, and his son, Richard, was eventually allowed to inherit first the duchy of York (after the death of his uncle) and some years later the earldom of March in right of his mother, Edmund Mortimer having died childless.

In 1461 the sentence against Richard of Conisbrough was one of those annulled by Edward IV's first Parliament. Richard has no surviving tomb, and although he was properly buried in Southampton, it's unlikely there was one in the first place. His widow, Maud survived until 1446 and is said to have lived at Conisbrough Castle, Turnham Hall and Sandal Castle.

SELECT BIBLIOGRAPHY

Calendar of Fine Rolls

Calendar of Close Rolls

Calendar of Patent Rolls

Dictionary of National Biography

Medieval London Widows, Edited by Caroline.M.Barron and Anne. F. Sutton

Complete Peerage, G.E. Cockayne

The Revolt of Owain Glyn Dwr, R.R. Davies

The Baronage in the Reign of Richard II, Keith E Fildes.

The Age of Richard II, edited by James L. Gillespie

Power Ambition and Reconciliation: The Despensers c1281-1400 (Unpublished PhD
Thesis, York), M. J. Lawrence

The Court of Richard II, Gervase Mathew

The Fears of Henry IV, Ian Mortimer

Henry V and the Southampton Plot, T.B. Pugh

Richard II, Nigel Saul

England in the Reign of Henry IV, I.H.Wylie

The Reign of Henry V, J.H.Wylie and W.T.Waugh

10044204R00028

Printed in Great Britain
by Amazon.co.uk, Ltd.,
Marston Gate.

LOW BLOOD PRESSURE COOKBOOK

350+ Heart-Healthy Meals To Improve Your Wellness
And Control Low Blood Pressure

By

Corniliour C. Mawren

TABLE OF CONTENT

INTRODUCTION:

Blood pressure is a vital health indicator, measuring the force exerted by the blood against the walls of the arteries as it circulates throughout the body. Low blood pressure, or hypotension, occurs when blood pressure falls below the normal range, leading to insufficient blood flow to vital organs. While low blood pressure may not always cause noticeable symptoms, it can sometimes have serious consequences. This comprehensive introduction to low blood pressure will discuss the causes, symptoms, potential health risks, and management strategies to help you better understand this often-overlooked health condition.

A regular blood pressure reading is typically around 120/80 mm Hg, although this may vary depending on age, sex, and overall health. Hypotension is generally defined as blood pressure below 90/60 mm Hg. However, what constitutes "too low" can differ between individuals, as some people may naturally have lower blood pressure without any adverse effects. It is essential to consider the presence of symptoms and overall health when evaluating whether low blood pressure is a cause for concern.

There are several types of low blood pressure, including orthostatic (or postural) hypotension, which occurs when blood pressure drops suddenly upon standing up, and neurally mediated hypotension, which is triggered by an abnormal nervous system response to prolonged standing or emotional stress. Chronic low blood pressure can also indicate an underlying medical condition, such as heart problems, hormonal imbalances, or neurological disorders.

Symptoms of low blood pressure may vary but can include dizziness, lightheadedness, fainting, blurred vision, nausea, fatigue, and confusion. When the blood pressure falls too low, the body may struggle to deliver adequate oxygen and nutrients to vital organs, increasing the risk of organ damage and, in extreme cases, shock – a life-threatening condition that requires immediate medical attention.

The causes of low blood pressure can be diverse, ranging from dehydration, prolonged bed rest, and certain medications to more serious underlying health conditions. Pregnancy, blood loss, and septic shock are also possible causes. To identify the root cause of hypotension, healthcare providers may employ various diagnostic tools, such as blood tests, electrocardiograms, stress tests, and a thorough medical history and physical examination.

Managing low blood pressure often involves addressing the underlying cause and making appropriate lifestyle and dietary adjustments. For instance, increasing fluid intake, consuming a balanced diet rich in essential nutrients, and incorporating regular exercise can help improve blood pressure levels. In cases where medications cause hypotension, adjusting or changing the prescription may be necessary. For individuals with orthostatic hypotension, simple measures such as standing up slowly, wearing *compression stockings, or using support when getting out of bed can help alleviate symptoms.*

In conclusion, low blood pressure, while often overlooked, can have significant health implications. Understanding its causes, symptoms, and potential risks is crucial for effectively identifying and managing the condition. By maintaining a healthy lifestyle, staying well-informed, and working closely with healthcare providers, individuals with low blood pressure can effectively manage their condition and minimize any adverse effects on their overall well-being.

CHAPTER :1 IMPORTANCE OF A BALANCED DIET

A balanced diet can be necessary for managing low blood pressure. It can help support cardiovascular health and give the body the nutrients needed to maintain proper blood pressure levels. Here are some ways a balanced diet can be beneficial for managing low blood pressure:

Maintaining A Healthy Weight:

Being overweight can strain the cardiovascular system, leading to high blood pressure. Eating a balanced diet rich in whole grains, lean protein, fruits, and vegetables can help maintain a healthy weight, which can help manage low blood pressure.

1. **Eat a balanced diet**: Eating a balanced diet that includes a variety of fruits, vegetables, whole grains, lean proteins, and healthy fats can help maintain a healthy weight. Avoiding processed and high-calorie foods and limiting sugar and saturated fats is essential.

2. **Practice portion control**: Overeating, even healthy food, can lead to weight gain. Using smaller plates and measuring portions can help manage calorie intake.

3. **Stay hydrated**: Drinking enough water can help manage hunger and support weight loss.

4. **Engage in regular physical activity**: Regular physical activity can help burn calories and support weight

management. Aim for at least 30 minutes of moderate exercise daily, such as brisk walking.

5. **Get enough sleep**: Lack of sleep can disrupt hormones that control hunger and appetite, leading to overeating and weight gain. Aim for 7-8 hours of sleep each night.

6. **Manage stress levels**: Stress can lead to overeating and weight gain. Finding healthy ways to manage stress, such as meditation or exercise, can support weight management.

Reducing Sodium Intake:

Too much sodium can cause the body to retain water, increasing blood pressure. Eating a balanced diet that is low in sodium can help manage blood pressure levels.

1. **Read food labels:** Food labels list the amount of sodium per serving, so it's essential to check the label before purchasing or consuming a product. Look for products that are low in sodium or have no added salt.

2. **Avoid processed foods**: Processed and packaged foods are often high in sodium, so limiting consumption of these products is essential. Choose fresh foods such as fruits, vegetables, and lean proteins.

3. **Cook at home**: Cooking meals at home allows for better control over sodium intake. Use herbs and spices to add flavor to meals instead of salt.

4. **Rinse canned foods**: Canned foods such as beans and vegetables can be high in sodium. Rinse these foods under water before consuming them to reduce their sodium content.

5. **Choose low-sodium alternatives**: Many low-sodium alternatives, such as low-sodium soy sauce and reduced-sodium broths, are available.

6. **Be mindful of condiments**: Condiments such as ketchup, mustard, and salad dressings can be high in sodium. Choose low-sodium versions or make your own at home using fresh ingredients.

Increasing Potassium Intake:

Potassium can help regulate blood pressure by counteracting the effects of sodium in the body. A balanced diet rich in potassium-rich foods like bananas, sweet potatoes, and spinach can help manage low blood pressure.

1. **Eat potassium-rich foods**: Foods high in potassium include bananas, sweet potatoes, spinach, avocado, beans, and yogurt. Incorporating these foods into your diet can help increase potassium intake.

2. **Choose whole foods**: Whole foods such as fruits, vegetables, and whole grains are generally higher in potassium than processed foods.

3. **Drink coconut water**: Coconut water is a natural source of potassium and can be a healthy way to increase potassium intake.

4. **Add herbs and spices**: Herbs and spices such as parsley, basil, and turmeric are good sources of potassium and can be added to meals to increase potassium intake.

5. **Take potassium supplements**: Potassium supplements can be an option for people who cannot get enough potassium through their diet. However, talking to a healthcare provider before starting any supplements is essential.

It's important to remember that consuming too much potassium can also negatively affect health, especially for those with certain health conditions such as kidney disease. Talking to a healthcare provider before making any significant changes to potassium intake is essential.

Consuming Healthy Fats:

Healthy fats, such as those in avocados, nuts, and olive oil, can help support cardiovascular health and manage low blood pressure.

1. **Nuts and seeds**: Nuts and seeds are a good source of healthy fats. Examples include almonds, walnuts, chia seeds, and flaxseeds.

2. **Fatty fish**: Fatty fish such as salmon, tuna, and sardines are a good source of omega-3 fatty acids, which can help support heart health and brain function.

3. **Avocado**: Avocado is a good source of monounsaturated fats, which can help support heart health.

4. **Olive oil**: Olive oil is a good source of monounsaturated fats and can be used in cooking or as a salad dressing.

5. **Coconut oil** contains medium-chain triglycerides, which can be used for energy and may help support weight management.

6. **Nut butter**: Nut butter such as almonds or peanut butter can be a good source of healthy fats.

It's important to remember that while healthy fats are beneficial, they are also high in calories. Consuming them in moderation is essential as part of a balanced diet.

Staying Hydrated:

Dehydration can cause blood pressure to drop. Drinking enough water and consuming fluids through foods like fruits and vegetables can help manage low blood pressure.

CHAPTER:2 FOODS TO INCLUDE

Incorporating specific foods into your diet can help manage low blood pressure. Some of these include:

1. **Leafy greens**: Rich in nutrients and antioxidants, leafy greens like spinach, kale, and Swiss chard provide essential vitamins and minerals to support overall health.

2. **Whole grains**: Whole grains like brown rice, quinoa, and whole wheat bread provide a steady energy source and help maintain blood sugar levels, preventing sudden drops in blood pressure.

3. **Nuts and seeds**: Almonds, walnuts, chia seeds, and flaxseeds are excellent sources of healthy fats, fiber, and protein that can improve blood pressure regulation.

4. **Legumes:** Beans, lentils, and chickpeas are packed with nutrients and can help improve blood pressure by providing a steady energy source and supporting healthy blood vessels.

CHAPTER :3 FOODS TO AVOID

While including certain foods can help manage low blood pressure, avoiding others is equally important. Some of the foods to limit or avoid include:

Salt:

Salt is a common ingredient in many foods, but consuming too much can be harmful, especially for individuals with low blood pressure. Consuming excess salt can cause the body to retain fluid, raising blood pressure and straining the heart and blood vessels.

It's recommended that individuals with low blood pressure limit their salt intake to no more than 2,300 milligrams per day. However, many processed and packaged foods contain high amounts of sodium, so it's important to read food labels and choose low-sodium options whenever possible.

There are also many ways to reduce salt intake while enjoying flavorful meals. For example, herbs, spices, and citrus juices instead of salt can add flavor without excess sodium. Cooking meals from scratch using fresh ingredients can also help reduce salt intake, as many processed and packaged foods are high in sodium.

Working with a healthcare provider to develop a personalized plan for managing low blood pressure and reducing salt intake is essential. Individuals with low blood pressure can help support cardiovascular health and overall well-being by making gradual and sustainable changes to one's diet and lifestyle.

Caffeine:

Caffeine is a stimulant that can positively and negatively affect blood pressure. In some individuals, caffeine can temporarily raise blood pressure, harming those with low blood pressure.

It's recommended that individuals with low blood pressure limit caffeine intake to no more than 200 milligrams per day, equivalent to about one 8-ounce cup of coffee. It's also important to note that the amount of caffeine in different foods and beverages can vary widely, so it's essential to be aware of the caffeine content of other products.

Some individuals may be more sensitive to the effects of caffeine than others and may need to limit caffeine intake even further. It's essential to monitor blood pressure levels and speak with a healthcare provider about any concerns related to caffeine consumption.

In addition to limiting caffeine intake, individuals with low blood pressure can also consider other strategies for managing blood pressure, such as engaging in regular physical activity, reducing salt intake, and consuming a balanced diet with plenty of fruits, vegetables, whole grains, lean proteins, and healthy fats.

Overall, limiting caffeine intake can be beneficial for managing low blood pressure and supporting overall cardiovascular health. Considering individual factors and working with a healthcare provider to develop a personalized plan for managing low blood pressure is essential.

Alcohol:

Alcohol can have adverse effects on blood pressure and cardiovascular health. Consuming excessive amounts of alcohol can raise blood pressure and increase the risk of developing cardiovascular disease. It's recommended that individuals with low blood pressure limit alcohol intake to no more than one drink per day for women and two for men.

Moderate alcohol consumption may have some health benefits, such as reducing the risk of heart disease. However, it's essential to consume alcohol in moderation and to consider other factors such as overall health status and family history of cardiovascular disease.

Additionally, some individuals may experience a temporary increase in blood pressure after consuming alcohol, which can harm those with low blood pressure. It's essential to monitor blood pressure levels and speak with a healthcare provider about any concerns related to alcohol consumption.

Overall, limiting alcohol intake and consuming it in moderation can be beneficial for managing low blood pressure and supporting overall cardiovascular health. Considering individual factors and working with a healthcare provider to develop a personalized plan for managing low blood pressure is essential.

High-Fat Foods:

High-fat foods, especially those that are high in saturated and trans fats, can have adverse effects on cardiovascular health and blood pressure. These types of fats can increase cholesterol levels and contribute to the development of cardiovascular disease.

It's recommended that individuals with low blood pressure limit their intake of saturated and trans fats and choose healthier sources such as monounsaturated and polyunsaturated fats. These fats can be found in nuts, seeds, avocados, fatty fish, and olive oil.

Choosing lean protein sources such as skinless chicken, fish, legumes, and low-fat dairy products is also essential. Limiting the intake of processed and packaged foods, often high in unhealthy fats, can also be beneficial for managing blood pressure and promoting overall health.

In addition to making dietary changes, engaging in regular physical activity, reducing salt intake, and limiting alcohol and caffeine consumption can also help manage low blood pressure.

Working with a healthcare provider to develop a personalized plan for managing low blood pressure and making lifestyle changes is essential. Individuals with low blood pressure can help support cardiovascular health and reduce the risk of chronic diseases by making gradual and sustainable changes to one's diet and lifestyle.

Processed And Packaged Foods:

Processed and packaged foods are often high in sodium, unhealthy fats, and added sugars, negatively affecting blood pressure and overall health. These foods can also be low in nutrients, contributing to nutrient deficiencies and poor health outcomes.

It's recommended that individuals with low blood pressure limit their intake of processed and packaged foods and choose whole, minimally processed foods whenever possible. Whole foods such as fruits, vegetables, whole grains, lean proteins, and healthy fats are nutrient-dense and can help support cardiovascular health.

When choosing packaged foods, it's important to read food labels and choose products low in sodium, unhealthy fats, and added sugars. Knowing serving sizes and portion control is essential, as many packaged foods contain multiple servings per container.

Cooking meals from scratch using fresh ingredients can also help reduce the intake of processed and packaged foods. This can be done by preparing meals ahead of time, using a slow cooker, or choosing quick and easy recipes that use whole, minimally processed foods.

In addition to making dietary changes, engaging in regular physical activity, reducing salt intake, and limiting alcohol and caffeine consumption can also help manage low blood pressure.

Working with a healthcare provider to develop a personalized plan for managing low blood pressure and making lifestyle changes is essential. Individuals with low blood pressure can help support cardiovascular health and reduce the risk of chronic diseases by making gradual and sustainable changes to one's diet and lifestyle.

CHAPTER:4 LIFESTYLE CHANGES

Lifestyle changes can be an effective way to manage low blood pressure and support overall health and well-being. In addition to dietary modifications, engaging in regular physical activity, getting enough sleep, and managing stress levels can all help manage low blood pressure.

Regular physical activity can help manage low blood pressure by improving cardiovascular health and increasing blood flow. Aim for at least 30 minutes of moderate-intensity exercise most days of the week. This can include brisk walking, cycling, swimming, or jogging. Speaking with a healthcare provider before starting a new exercise program is essential.

Getting enough sleep is also essential for managing low blood pressure. Lack of sleep can increase stress hormones, which can raise blood pressure. Aim for at least 7-8 hours of sleep per night and develop healthy sleep habits such as limiting caffeine intake, avoiding electronic devices before bed, and establishing a consistent sleep schedule.

Managing stress levels is also essential for managing low blood pressure. Chronic stress can increase blood pressure and have adverse effects on cardiovascular health. Stress-reducing activities such as yoga, meditation, or deep breathing exercises can help manage stress levels. It's also essential to identify and manage sources of stress in daily life.

Quitting smoking and limiting alcohol intake can also help manage low blood pressure. Smoking can constrict blood vessels and increase blood pressure, while excessive alcohol consumption can raise blood pressure and negatively affect cardiovascular health.

Working with a healthcare provider to develop a personalized plan for managing low blood pressure and making lifestyle changes is essential. Individuals with low blood pressure can help support cardiovascular health and reduce the risk of chronic diseases by making gradual and sustainable changes to one's diet and lifestyle.

In summary, lifestyle changes such as engaging in regular physical activity, getting enough sleep, managing stress levels, quitting smoking, and limiting alcohol intake can all be effective ways to manage low blood pressure. It's important to make gradual and sustainable changes to one's lifestyle and work with a healthcare provider to develop a personalized plan for managing low blood pressure. By making these changes, individuals with low blood pressure can help support cardiovascular health and overall well-being.

In addition to dietary modifications, incorporating healthy lifestyle habits can help manage low blood pressure. Some suggestions include the following:

1. **Regular exercise**: Physical activity can help improve blood circulation and strengthen your cardiovascular system.

2. **Eating smaller, more frequent meals**: Consuming smaller meals throughout the day can help prevent sudden drops in blood pressure.

3. **Monitoring your blood pressure**: Regularly check your blood pressure levels and consult your healthcare provider to ensure you maintain a healthy range.

CHAPTER:5 BREAKFAST RECIPE

Quinoa And Vegetable Breakfast Bowl:

Ingredients:
- 1 cup cooked quinoa
- 1/2 cup sautéed vegetables (such as bell peppers, onions, and mushrooms)
- 1 poached egg
- 1 tablespoon chopped fresh herbs (such as parsley, chives, or basil)
- Salt and pepper to taste

Instructions:
1. Follow the steps on the package to cook quinoa.
2. Sauté your pick of vegetables in a pan until tender.
3. Put an egg in water that cooks for 3 to 4 minutes.
4. In a bowl, mix the cooked quinoa and the cooked veggies.
5. Put the egg that was poached on top.
6. Salt and pepper to taste, then sprinkle with fresh herbs.

Almond Butter And Banana Toast:

Ingredients:

- 1 slice whole grain bread
- 1 tablespoon almond butter
- 1/2 banana, sliced
- 1 teaspoon honey
- Cinnamon (optional)

Instructions:

1. Toast the bread until it gets crunchy.
2. Almond butter should be spread on the toast.
3. Slice a banana and place it on top of the nut butter.
4. Pour honey over the slices of banana.
5. Cinnamon can be added if you want.

Greek Yogurt And Berry Parfait:

Ingredients:

- 1 cup Greek yogurt
- 1/2 cup mixed berries (such as strawberries, blueberries, and raspberries)
- 1/4 cup granola
- 1 tablespoon honey

Instructions:

1. Layer the Greek yogurt, mixed berries, and granola in a glass or bowl.
2. Honey should be poured on top.
3. Serve right away.

Spinach And Feta Egg Scramble:

Ingredients:

- 3 eggs
- 1/4 cup crumbled feta cheese
- 1/2 cup fresh spinach leaves, chopped
- 1 tablespoon olive oil
- Salt and pepper to taste

Instructions:

1. With a fork, beat the eggs together in a small bowl.
2. In a pan, heat the olive oil over medium heat.
3. Add the eggs that have been beaten and the chopped spinach to the pan.
4. Scramble the eggs with a spoon and cook until they are set.
5. Crumble feta cheese and sprinkle it on top of the cooking eggs.
6. Salt and pepper can be added to taste.

Chia Seed Pudding With Fresh Fruit:

Ingredients:

- 1/4 cup chia seeds
- 1 cup almond milk
- 1 tablespoon honey
- 1/2 cup fresh fruit (such as sliced strawberries, blueberries, and raspberries)
- 1 tablespoon chopped nuts (such as almonds or walnuts)

Instructions:

1. In a bowl, combine the chia seeds, almond milk, and honey by whisking them together.

2. Cover the bowl and put it in the fridge overnight or for at least 4 hours.
3. Stir the chia seed pudding before serving to ensure the seeds are spread evenly.
4. Add fresh fruit and chopped nuts to the top.

Overnight Oats With Nuts And Berries:

Ingredients:
- 1/2 cup rolled oats
- 1/2 cup almond milk
- 1/4 cup mixed berries (such as sliced strawberries, blueberries, and raspberries)
- 1 tablespoon chopped nuts (such as almonds or walnuts)
- 1 tablespoon honey

Instructions:
1. Mix the rolled oats, almond milk, and honey in a jar or bowl.
2. Put a lid on the jar or bowl in the fridge overnight.
3. In the morning, stir the oats to ensure the milk is evenly spread.
4. Add mixed berries and chopped nuts to the top.

Whole Wheat Avocado Toast:

Ingredients:
- 1 slice whole wheat bread
- 1/2 avocado, sliced
- 1/2 lime, juiced
- Salt and pepper to taste

Instructions:

1. Toast the bread until it gets crunchy.
2. Use a fork to mash the chopped avocado, then mix in the lime juice.
3. Spread the avocado spread on the bread that has been toasted.
4. Salt and pepper can be added to taste.

Hearty Oatmeal With Cinnamon And Apples:

Ingredients:

- 1/2 cup rolled oats
- 1 cup water or milk
- 1 apple, chopped
- 1 teaspoon cinnamon
- 1 tablespoon honey
- 1 tablespoon chopped nuts (such as almonds or walnuts)

Instructions:

1. Bring water or milk to a boil in a pot.
2. Pour the chopped apple and rolled oats into the boiling liquid.
3. Turn down the heat and let the oats simmer until they are soft and the beverage is consumed.
4. Mix in honey and cinnamon.
5. Add chopped nuts on top.

Veggie Omelette With Whole Grain Bread:

Ingredients:

- 2 eggs
- 1/2 cup chopped vegetables (such as bell peppers, onions, and mushrooms)
- 1 tablespoon olive oil
- Salt and pepper to taste
- 1 slice whole grain bread

Instructions:

1. With a fork, beat the eggs together in a small bowl.
2. In a pan, heat the olive oil over medium heat.
3. Put the chopped veggies in the pan and cook them until soft.
4. Pour the beaten eggs on the cooked veggies and cook until the eggs are set.
5. Fold the egg in half with a spatula.
6. Salt and pepper can be added to taste.
7. Serve with a slice of bread made with whole grains.

Smoked Salmon And Cream Cheese Bagel:

Ingredients:

- 1 whole grain bagel, sliced
- 2 tablespoons cream cheese
- 2 slices smoked salmon
- 1 tablespoon capers
- 1 tablespoon chopped fresh dill

Instructions:

1. Toast the toast until it gets crunchy.
2. On the warm bagel, spread cream cheese.
3. On top of the cream cheese, put the smoked salmon.
4. Sprinkle the top with olives and fresh dill.

Ricotta And Honey Toast With Walnuts:

Ingredients:

- 1 slice whole grain bread
- 2 tablespoons ricotta cheese
- 1 tablespoon honey
- 1 tablespoon chopped walnuts

Instructions:

1. Toast the bread until it gets crunchy.
2. Ricotta cheese should be spread on the toast.
3. Honey goes well with ricotta cheese.
4. On top, sprinkle chopped walnuts.

Blueberry Almond Smoothie Bowl:

Ingredients:

- 1 cup almond milk
- 1 banana, sliced
- 1/2 cup frozen blueberries
- 1/4 cup rolled oats
- 1 tablespoon almond butter
- 1 teaspoon honey
- 1 tablespoon chopped almonds
- 1 tablespoon chia seeds

Instructions:

1. Mix the almond milk, banana, frozen blueberries, rolled oats, almond butter, and honey in a mixer.
2. Mix until it's smooth.
3. The drink should go into a bowl.
4. Almonds and chia seeds are sprinkled on top.

Shakshuka With Whole Wheat Pita:

Ingredients:

- 2 eggs
- 1/2 cup canned tomatoes
- 1/4 cup chopped bell peppers
- 1/4 cup chopped onions
- 1 clove garlic, minced
- 1/2 teaspoon paprika
- Salt and pepper to taste
- 1 whole wheat pita, toasted

Instructions:

1. Heat the canned tomatoes, bell peppers, onions, and garlic over medium heat in a small pot.
2. Mix in the paprika and season to taste with salt and pepper.
3. Put eggs in the pot and cover it with the lid.
4. Cook for about 5 minutes or until the eggs are set.
5. Serve with toasted bread made from whole wheat.

Protein-Packed Breakfast Burrito:

Ingredients:

- 1 whole wheat tortilla
- 2 eggs, scrambled
- 1/4 cup black beans
- 1/4 cup shredded cheddar cheese
- 1 tablespoon salsa
- 1 tablespoon chopped cilantro

Instructions:

1. In a small pan, beat eggs until set.
2. Put the scrambled eggs, black beans, sliced cheddar cheese, salsa, and chopped cilantro in the middle of a whole wheat tortilla.
3. Make a burrito by rolling up the dough.

Turkey And Spinach Breakfast Sandwich:

Ingredients:

- 1 whole grain English muffin, sliced and toasted
- 2 slices turkey breast
- 1/4 cup fresh spinach leaves
- 1 egg, fried
- Salt and pepper to taste

Instructions:

1. The English muffin pieces should be toasted until they are crisp.
2. Layer the turkey breast and fresh spinach leaves on one of the warmed English muffin halves.

3. In a small pan, cook an egg until it is set.
4. On top of the spinach leaves, put the fried egg.
5. Salt and pepper can be added to taste.
6. Place the other half of the warm English muffin on top.

Cottage Cheese And Pineapple Bowl:

Ingredients:

- 1/2 cup low-fat cottage cheese
- 1/2 cup fresh pineapple chunks
- 1 tablespoon chopped almonds
- 1 teaspoon honey

Instructions:

1. Mix the low-fat cottage cheese and fresh pineapple chunks in a bowl.
2. Honey should be poured on top.
3. Sprinkle the top with chopped nuts.

Baked Egg And Vegetable Muffins:

Ingredients:

- 6 eggs
- 1/2 cup chopped vegetables (such as bell peppers, onions, and mushrooms)
- 1/4 cup shredded cheddar cheese
- Salt and pepper to taste

Instructions:

1. Set oven temperature to 350°F (175°C).
2. Whisk eggs with salt and pepper in a bowl.
3. Put chopped veggies and shredded cheddar cheese into the bowl.

4. Pour the egg mix into a muffin tin that has been greased.
5. Bake for 15 to 20 minutes or until the eggs are set.
6. Take it out of the oven and let it cool for 5 minutes before you serve it.

Apple Cinnamon Quinoa Porridge:

Ingredients:

- 1 cup cooked quinoa
- 1 cup almond milk
- 1 apple, peeled and chopped
- 1/2 teaspoon cinnamon
- 1 tablespoon honey

Instructions:

1. Mix the cooked rice, almond milk, chopped apple, and cinnamon in a saucepan.
2. Bring to a simmer and cook, turning now and then, until the mixture thickens.
3. Stir in the honey, and keep cooking the rice until it is warm all the way through.
4. Prepare hot.

Nutty Granola With Yogurt And Fruit:

Ingredients:

- 1 cup plain Greek yogurt
- 1/2 cup nutty granola (store-bought or homemade)
- 1/2 cup mixed fruit (such as sliced strawberries, blueberries, and raspberries)
- 1 tablespoon honey

Instructions:

1. Mix Greek yogurt and honey in a bowl.
2. Put the crunchy granola on top of the yogurt.
3. Add mixed fruit to the top.

Banana, Oat, And Nut Pancakes:

Ingredients:

- 1 ripe banana, mashed
- 1/2 cup rolled oats
- 2 tablespoons chopped nuts (such as almonds or walnuts)
- 1 egg
- 1/4 cup almond milk
- 1/4 teaspoon cinnamon
- 1/4 teaspoon vanilla extract
- Maple syrup (optional)

Instructions:

1. Blend the mashed banana, rolled oats, chopped nuts, egg, almond milk, cinnamon, and vanilla extract.
2. Heat a pan that doesn't stick on medium heat.
3. Spoon the pancake batter onto the pan to make about 3 inches in diameter pancake.
4. Cook for about 2 to 3 minutes, or until bubbles form on the top of the pancakes and the edges start to dry out.
5. Flip the pancakes and cook for another minute or two.
6. If you want, serve it with maple syrup.

Warm Barley Salad With Roasted Vegetables:

Ingredients:

- 1 cup cooked barley
- 1/2 cup roasted vegetables (such as bell peppers, onions, and zucchini)
- 1/4 cup crumbled feta cheese
- 1 tablespoon chopped fresh herbs (such as parsley, chives, or basil)
- Salt and pepper to taste
- 1 tablespoon olive oil

Instructions:

1. Set oven temperature to 400°F (200°C).
2. Mix the roasted veggies with olive oil, salt, and pepper in a bowl.
3. Spread the veggies in a single layer on a baking sheet, and roast them in the oven for 20 to 25 minutes or until soft and lightly browned.
4. Mix the cooked barley and the roasted vegetables in a separate bowl.
5. Crumbled feta cheese should be sprinkled on top.
6. Salt and pepper can be added to taste.
7. Add chopped fresh herbs to the top. Warm is best.

Lentil And Vegetable Breakfast Hash:

Ingredients:

- 1 cup cooked lentils
- 1/2 cup chopped vegetables (such as bell peppers, onions, and mushrooms)
- 1 tablespoon olive oil
- 1/4 teaspoon smoked paprika
- Salt and pepper to taste
- 1 egg (optional)

Instructions:

1. In a pan, heat the olive oil over medium heat.
2. Add the chopped veggies and cook them until they are soft.
3. Add cooked beans and smoked paprika to the mixture.
4. Cook the lentils until they are hot all the way through.
5. If you want, you can fry an egg in a different pan.
6. Serve the fried egg on top of the lentil and veggie hash.

Banana And Almond Butter Smoothie:

Ingredients:

- 1 banana, sliced
- 1 tablespoon almond butter
- 1/2 cup almond milk
- 1/2 cup ice
- 1/2 teaspoon vanilla extract
- 1/4 teaspoon cinnamon

Instructions:

1. Mix the banana slices, almond butter, almond milk, ice, vanilla flavor, and cinnamon in a blender.
2. Mix until it's smooth.
3. Serve right away.

Veggie Frittata With Whole Wheat Toast:

Ingredients:

- 2 eggs
- 1/2 cup chopped vegetables (such as bell peppers, onions, and mushrooms)
- 1 tablespoon olive oil
- Salt and pepper to taste
- 1 slice whole wheat toast

Instructions:

1. Set oven temperature to 350°F (175°C).

2. Heat the olive oil over medium heat in a small pan that can go in the oven.

3. Add the chopped veggies and cook them until they are soft.

4. In a small bowl, beat the eggs and add salt and pepper to taste.

5. Pour the eggs into the pan where the veggies are cooking.

6. Cook the frittata for 2 to 3 minutes or until the bottom is set.

7. Put the pan in the oven and bake for 5 to 7 minutes or until the frittata is done.

8. Serve with a slice of toast made from whole wheat.

Mixed Berry And Chia Seed Parfait:

Ingredients:
- 1/2 cup plain Greek yogurt
- 1/4 cup mixed berries (such as strawberries, blueberries, and raspberries)
- 1 tablespoon chia seeds
- 1 teaspoon honey

Instructions:
1. Combine the regular Greek yogurt, chia seeds, and honey in a bowl.

2. Put some yogurt mixture in the bottom of a glass or bowl.

3. Add a layer of mixed berries on top.

4. Layer more yogurt and berries until all the items are gone.
5. Refrigerate for at least 30 minutes before serving.

Avocado And Egg Breakfast Tacos:

Ingredients:
- 2 corn tortillas
- 2 eggs
- 1/2 avocado, sliced
- 1/4 cup chopped tomatoes
- Salt and pepper to taste
- 1 tablespoon olive oil

Instructions:
1. In a small pan, heat the olive oil over medium heat.
2. Salt and pepper to taste, then break eggs into the pan.
3. Fry eggs until the whites are set, but the yolks are still runny.
4. Tortillas can be heated in a different pan or the microwave.
5. Put the fried eggs on top of the bread to make the tacos.
6. Avocado slices and tomato chunks go on top.

Spiced Chickpea And Spinach Scramble:

Ingredients:

- 2 eggs
- 1/2 cup cooked chickpeas
- 1/2 cup fresh spinach leaves
- 1/4 teaspoon cumin powder
- 1/4 teaspoon paprika
- Salt and pepper to taste
- 1 tablespoon olive oil

Instructions:

1. In a bowl, whisk the eggs with the cumin powder, paprika, salt, and pepper.
2. In a pan, heat the olive oil over medium heat.
3. Add the cooked beans to the pan and cook for two to three minutes.
4. Put some fresh spinach leaves in the pan and cook them until soft.
5. Pour the egg mixture over the chickpeas and spinach into the pan.
6. Cook the eggs, stirring every so often, until they are set.
7. Prepare hot.

Warm Millet Breakfast Bowl With Fruit:

Ingredients:

- 1/2 cup cooked millet
- 1/4 cup mixed fruit (such as sliced peaches, strawberries, and blueberries)
- 1 tablespoon chopped nuts (such as almonds or walnuts)
- 1 teaspoon honey

Instructions:

1. Mix cooked millet and honey in a bowl.
2. Put a spoonful of mixed fruit on the millet.
3. Add some chopped nuts on top.
4. Microwave the fruit for one to two minutes or until it is warm.

Whole Grain Waffles With Fresh Berries:

Ingredients:

- 1 cup whole wheat flour
- 1 tablespoon baking powder
- 1/4 teaspoon salt
- 1 cup almond milk
- 2 eggs
- 1 tablespoon honey
- 1 teaspoon vanilla extract
- Fresh berries for serving

Instructions:

1. Follow the directions on the waffle iron box to heat it.
2. Whisk together the whole wheat flour, baking powder, and salt
3. in a bowl.
4. Whisk together almond milk, eggs, honey, and vanilla extract in a different bowl.
5. Pour the liquids into the dry ingredients and stir until everything is well-mixed.
6. Put the batter on the waffle pan and cook it according to the instructions on the package.
7. Put fresh berries on top before serving.

Multigrain Muesli With Almond Milk:

Ingredients:
- 1/2 cup multigrain cereal
- 1/4 cup chopped nuts (such as almonds or walnuts)
- 1/4 cup mixed dried fruit (such as raisins, cranberries, and apricots)
- 1/2 cup almond milk
- 1 teaspoon honey

Instructions:
1. Mix cereal with different grains, chopped nuts, and dried fruit in a bowl.
2. Honey should be poured on top.
3. Almond milk should be poured on top.

4. Let the cereal sit for 5–10 minutes to soften up before serving.

CHAPTER:6 LUNCH RECIPES

Grilled Chicken And Quinoa Salad:

Ingredients:

- 1 chicken breast, grilled and sliced
- 1/2 cup cooked quinoa
- 1/4 cup chopped vegetables (such as bell peppers, onions, and cucumbers)
- 1 tablespoon chopped fresh herbs (such as parsley or basil)
- Salt and pepper to taste
- 1 tablespoon olive oil

Instructions:

1. Mix cooked quinoa, chopped veggies, and fresh herbs in a bowl.
2. Salt and pepper can be added to taste.
3. Pour olive oil on top and mix with your hands.
4. Sliced grilled chicken goes on top.

Lentil And Vegetable Soup:

Ingredients:

- 1 cup cooked lentils
- 1/2 cup chopped vegetables (such as carrots, celery, and onions)
- 1 tablespoon olive oil
- 1 clove garlic, minced
- 1/4 teaspoon cumin powder
- 1/4 teaspoon paprika
- Salt and pepper to taste
- 2 cups vegetable broth

Instructions:

1. Olive oil should be heated in a pot on medium heat.
2. Put chopped veggies and minced garlic in the bank and cook until the vegetables are soft.
3. Mix in the lentils that have been cooked, cumin powder, paprika, salt, and pepper.
4. Pour vegetable broth on top of the lentils and veggies.
5. Bring to a boil, then turn down the heat and simmer for 10 to 15 minutes or until the veggies are soft.
6. Prepare hot.

Turkey And Avocado Wrap:

Ingredients:

- 1 whole wheat wrap
- 2 slices turkey breast
- 1/2 avocado, sliced
- 1/4 cup chopped vegetables (such as bell peppers, onions, and tomatoes)
- Salt and pepper to taste
- 1 tablespoon mayonnaise (optional)

Instructions:

1. Put the flat whole wheat wrap on a plate.
2. If you want to use it, spread mayonnaise in the middle of the wrap.
3. On top of the mayonnaise, put slices of turkey breast.
4. Avocado slices and chopped veggies go on top.
5. Salt and pepper can be added to taste.
6. Fold the sides of the wrap in, then tightly roll it up.
7. Half the slice and serve.

Spinach And Goat Cheese Stuffed Portobello Mushrooms:

Ingredients:

- 2 portobello mushroom caps
- 1 cup fresh spinach leaves
- 1/4 cup crumbled goat cheese
- 1 clove garlic, minced
- Salt and pepper to taste
- 1 tablespoon olive oil

Instructions:

1. Set oven temperature to 375°F (190°C).
2. Take the stems off the portobello mushroom caps and scrape the guts with a spoon.
3. Mix fresh spinach leaves, chopped goat cheese, minced garlic, salt, and pepper in a bowl.
4. Fill the mushroom caps with a mix of spinach and goat cheese.
5. Put the mushroom caps that have been filled on a baking sheet.
6. Olive oil should be drizzled over the mushroom caps.
7. Bake in the oven for 20 to 25 minutes or until the mushrooms are soft and the sauce is hot and bubbling.
8. Prepare hot.

Tuna And White Bean Salad:

Ingredients:

- 1 can of tuna, drained and flaked
- 1/2 cup cooked white beans
- 1/4 cup chopped vegetables (such as bell peppers, onions, and celery)
- 1 tablespoon chopped fresh herbs (such as parsley or dill)
- Salt and pepper to taste
- 1 tablespoon olive oil

Instructions:

1. Combine tuna chunks, cooked white beans, chopped veggies, and fresh herbs in a bowl.
2. Salt and pepper can be added to taste.
3. Pour olive oil on top and mix with your hands.
4. Cool and serve.

Mediterranean Couscous Salad:

Ingredients:

- 1 cup cooked couscous
- 1/2 cup chopped vegetables (such as tomatoes, cucumbers, and red onions)
- 1/4 cup crumbled feta cheese
- 1/4 cup chopped fresh herbs (such as parsley or mint)
- Salt and pepper to taste
- 1 tablespoon olive oil

- 1 tablespoon lemon juice

Instructions:

1. Mix cooked couscous, chopped veggies, crumbled feta cheese, and fresh herbs in a bowl.
2. Salt and pepper can be added to taste.
3. Pour olive oil and lemon juice over the top, then toss everything together.
4. Cool and serve.

Sweet Potato And Black Bean Burrito Bowl:

Ingredients:

- 1 medium sweet potato, peeled and cubed
- 1/2 cup cooked black beans
- 1/4 cup chopped vegetables (such as bell peppers, onions, and tomatoes)
- 1/4 teaspoon chili powder
- Salt and pepper to taste
- 1 tablespoon olive oil
- 1/2 cup cooked brown rice
- Salsa and avocado for serving

Instructions:

1. Set oven temperature to 375°F (190°C).
2. Mix olive oil, chili powder, salt, and pepper with cut sweet potatoes.
3. Spread sweet potato cubes in a single layer on a baking sheet, and roast them in the oven for 20 to 25 minutes or until soft.

4. In a bowl, stir together cooked black beans, chopped veggies, salt, and pepper.
5. Put cooked brown rice in a bowl to make the burrito bowl.
6. Top with black bean and sweet potato cubes that have been roasted.
7. Add salsa and avocado before serving.

Chickpea And Vegetable Stir-Fry:

Ingredients:

- 1 can of chickpeas, drained and rinsed
- 1/2 cup chopped vegetables (such as bell peppers, onions, and broccoli)
- 1 tablespoon olive oil
- 1 clove garlic, minced
- 1/4 teaspoon cumin powder
- 1/4 teaspoon paprika
- Salt and pepper to taste
- 1 tablespoon soy sauce
- Cooked brown rice for serving

Instructions:

1. In a pan, heat the olive oil over medium heat.
2. Put chopped veggies and minced garlic in the pan and cook until the vegetables are soft.
3. Mix in the beans that have been drained and rinsed, cumin powder, paprika, salt, and pepper.
4. Cook the chickpeas for 2 to 3 minutes or until they are hot.
5. Pour some soy sauce on top and stir it all together. Dark rice that has been cooked.

Shrimp And Avocado Salad With Citrus Dressing:

Ingredients:

- 1 cup cooked shrimp, peeled and deveined
- 1 avocado, sliced
- 1/4 cup chopped vegetables (such as bell peppers, onions, and tomatoes)
- 1 tablespoon chopped fresh herbs (such as cilantro or parsley)
- Salt and pepper to taste
- 1 tablespoon olive oil
- 1 tablespoon fresh lime juice
- 1/2 teaspoon honey

Instructions:

1. Mix cooked shrimp, avocado slices, chopped veggies, and fresh herbs in a bowl.
2. Salt and pepper can be added to taste.
3. Whisk together olive oil, lime juice, and honey in a different bowl to make the citrus dressing.
4. Pour the lemon dressing over the shrimp and avocado, then toss everything together.
5. Cool and serve.

Caprese Salad Sandwich:

Ingredients:
- 2 slices of whole wheat bread
- 2 pieces of mozzarella cheese
- 1 large tomato, sliced
- 1/4 cup fresh basil leaves
- Salt and pepper to taste
- 1 tablespoon balsamic glaze
- 1 tablespoon olive oil

Instructions:
1. Toast the slices of whole wheat bread.
2. On top of one of the toasted bread pieces, put slices of mozzarella cheese, slices of tomato, and fresh basil leaves.
3. Salt and pepper can be added to taste.
4. Pour balsamic sauce over the slices of tomato.
5. Make a sandwich by putting the other slice of warmed bread on the filling.
6. Coat the outside of the sandwich with olive oil.
7. Heat a pan over medium heat, then cook the sandwich for 2 to 3 minutes on each side or until the cheese is melted and the bread is golden brown.
8. Prepare hot.

Roasted Red Pepper And Hummus Pita:

Ingredients:

- 1 whole wheat pita bread
- 1/4 cup roasted red peppers, sliced
- 2 tablespoons hummus
- 1/4 cup chopped vegetables (such as cucumber, red onion, and lettuce)
- Salt and pepper to taste

Instructions:

1. You can make two boxes by cutting the whole wheat pita bread in half.
2. Spread hummus in each pocket of pita bread.
3. Fill each pocket with red pepper slices and chopped veggies roasted.
4. Salt and pepper can be added to taste.
5. Serve right away.

Egg Salad Lettuce Wraps:

Ingredients:

- 2 hard-boiled eggs, chopped
- 1/4 cup chopped vegetables (such as celery and red onion)
- 1 tablespoon mayonnaise
- Salt and pepper to taste
- 4 large lettuce leaves

Instructions:

1. Mix chopped hard-boiled eggs, chopped veggies, mayonnaise, salt, and pepper in a bowl.
2. Lay giant lettuce leaves flat on a plate.
3. Put a spoonful of the egg salad mixture in the middle of each lettuce leaf.
4. Fold the sides of the lettuce leaf in, and then tightly roll it up.
5. Half the slice and serve.

Greek Salad With Grilled Chicken:

Ingredients:
- 1 chicken breast, grilled and sliced
- 1/2 cup chopped vegetables (such as cucumber, cherry tomatoes, and red onion)
- 1/4 cup crumbled feta cheese
- 1/4 cup pitted kalamata olives
- 1 tablespoon chopped fresh herbs (such as oregano or parsley)
- Salt and pepper to taste
- 1 tablespoon olive oil
- 1 tablespoon red wine vinegar

Instructions:
1. Mix chopped veggies, crumbled feta cheese, kalamata olives with the pits removed, and fresh herbs in a bowl.
2. Salt and pepper can be added to taste.
3. Pour olive oil and red wine vinegar over the top and mix with your hands.
4. Sliced grilled chicken goes on top.

Sesame Noodle Salad With Tofu:

Ingredients:

- 8 oz. whole wheat spaghetti
- 1/2 cup sliced vegetables (such as bell peppers, carrots, and cucumbers)
- 1/4 cup chopped fresh herbs (such as cilantro or parsley)
- 1/4 cup toasted sesame seeds
- Salt and pepper to taste
- 1 tablespoon olive oil
- 1 tablespoon soy sauce
- 1 tablespoon honey
- 1 tablespoon rice vinegar
- 1/2 block of firm tofu, drained and cubed

Instructions:

1. Follow the directions on the package to cook whole wheat spaghetti.
2. Mix together sliced veggies, chopped fresh herbs, and toasted sesame seeds in a bowl.
3. Salt and pepper can be added to taste.
4. The dressing is made by whisking together olive oil, soy sauce, honey, and rice vinegar in a different bowl.
5. Rinse cooked spaghetti with cold water after you drain it.
6. Put spaghetti in the bowl with the herbs and veggies.
7. Add tofu cubes to the bowl.
8. Pour the sauce on top and toss everything together.
9. Cool and serve.

Quinoa And Vegetable Stuffed Peppers:

Ingredients:

- 2 bell peppers, halved and seeded
- 1 cup cooked quinoa
- 1/2 cup chopped vegetables (such as onions, mushrooms, and zucchini)

- 1/4 cup chopped fresh herbs (such as parsley or cilantro)
- Salt and pepper to taste
- 1 tablespoon olive oil
- 1/4 cup shredded cheese (such as cheddar or mozzarella)

Instructions:
1. Set oven temperature to 375°F (190°C).
2. Mix the cooked quinoa, the chopped veggies, the chopped fresh herbs, the salt, and the pepper in a bowl.
3. Pour olive oil over the mixture and mix it up with your hands.
4. Stuff the quinoa and veggie mix into the bell peppers cut in half.
5. Shredded cheese goes on top of each pepper.
6. Put the peppers that have been stuffed on a baking sheet.
7. Bake for 20–25 minutes until the peppers are soft and the cheese is bubbling and melting. Prepare hot.

Falafel Salad With Tahini Dressing:

Ingredients:
- 4 falafel balls, cooked and crumbled
- 2 cups mixed greens
- 1/2 cup chopped vegetables (such as cucumber, cherry tomatoes, and red onion)
- 2 tablespoons chopped fresh herbs (such as parsley or mint)
- Salt and pepper to taste
- 1 tablespoon olive oil
- 1 tablespoon lemon juice
- 1 tablespoon tahini
- 1 clove garlic, minced

Instructions:

1. Combine broken-up falafel balls, mixed greens, chopped veggies, and fresh herbs in a bowl.
2. Salt and pepper can be added to taste.
3. The dressing is made by whisking together olive oil, lemon juice, tahini, and minced garlic in a separate bowl.
4. Pour the sauce over the salad and mix it all.
5. Cool and serve.

Chicken Caesar Salad With Whole Grain Croutons:

Ingredients:

- 2 cups mixed greens
- 1 cooked chicken breast, sliced
- 1/4 cup whole grain croutons
- 2 tablespoons grated Parmesan cheese
- Salt and pepper to taste
- 1 tablespoon olive oil
- 1 tablespoon lemon juice
- 1 clove garlic, minced
- 1/2 teaspoon Dijon mustard

Instructions:

1. Mix mixed veggies, cooked chicken breast slices, croutons made from whole grains, and grated Parmesan cheese in a bowl.
2. Salt and pepper can be added to taste.
3. The Caesar sauce is made by whisking together olive oil, lemon juice, minced garlic, and Dijon mustard in a separate bowl.
4. Pour the Caesar sauce over the salad and toss it to mix it all.
5. Cool and serve.

Gazpacho With Whole Wheat Bread:

Ingredients:

- 4 large tomatoes, roughly chopped
- 1/2 cucumber, roughly chopped
- 1/2 red bell pepper, roughly chopped
- 1/2 red onion, roughly chopped
- 1 clove garlic, minced
- 2 tablespoons olive oil
- 1 tablespoon red wine vinegar
- Salt and pepper to taste
- Whole wheat bread, sliced

Instructions:

1. Mix chopped tomatoes, cucumber, red bell pepper, red onion, and minced garlic until smooth.
2. Pour the ingredients into a big bowl.
3. Add olive oil and red wine vinegar and mix well.
4. Salt and pepper can be added to taste.
5. Before you serve the gazpacho, put it in the fridge for at least 30 minutes.
6. Serve cold with whole-wheat bread slices.

Broccoli And Cheddar Stuffed Sweet Potatoes:

Ingredients:

- 2 medium sweet potatoes
- 1 cup chopped broccoli florets
- 1/2 cup shredded cheddar cheese
- Salt and pepper to taste
- 1 tablespoon olive oil

Instructions:

1. Set oven temperature to 400°F (200°C).
2. Use a fork to poke holes all over the sweet potatoes.

3. Put the sweet potatoes on a baking sheet and bake them for 45 minutes to an hour or until soft.
4. In a skillet, cook chopped broccoli sprouts in olive oil over medium heat until smooth.
5. You can open the baked sweet potatoes and put cooked broccoli and chopped cheddar cheese inside.
6. Salt and pepper can be added to taste.
7. Put the stuffed sweet potatoes back in the oven and bake for 5–10 minutes or until the cheese is melted and bubbly.
8. Prepare hot.

Asian Chicken Salad With Peanut Dressing:

Ingredients:

- 1 cooked chicken breast, sliced
- 2 cups mixed greens
- 1/2 cup chopped vegetables (such as cucumber, carrots, and red cabbage)
- 2 tablespoons chopped fresh herbs (such as cilantro or mint)
- Salt and pepper to taste
- 1 tablespoon olive oil
- 1 tablespoon rice vinegar
- 1 tablespoon soy sauce
- 1 tablespoon honey
- 1/4 cup creamy peanut butter
- 1 clove garlic, minced

Instructions:

1. Mix cooked chicken breast slices, mixed greens, chopped veggies, and fresh herbs in a bowl.
2. Salt and pepper can be added to taste.
3. The peanut dressing is made by whisking together olive oil, rice vinegar, soy sauce, honey, creamy peanut butter, and chopped garlic in a separate bowl.

4. Pour the peanut sauce over the salad and mix it all.
5. Cool and serve.

Pesto Pasta Salad With Cherry Tomatoes:

Ingredients:
- 8 oz. whole wheat pasta
- 1 cup cherry tomatoes, halved
- 1/2 cup chopped vegetables (such as bell peppers and red onion)
- 2 tablespoons chopped fresh herbs (such as basil or parsley)
- Salt and pepper to taste
- 1/4 cup pesto
- 2 tablespoons olive oil
- 1 tablespoon lemon juice

Instructions:
1. Follow the directions on the package to cook whole wheat pasta.
2. Rinse cooked pasta with cold water after you drain it.
3. Mix cooked pasta, cherry tomatoes, chopped veggies, chopped fresh herbs, salt, and pepper in a bowl.
4. The dressing is made by whisking pesto, olive oil, and lemon juice in a separate bowl.
5. Pour the sauce over the pasta salad and mix it.
6. Cool and serve.

Turkey, Apple, And Brie Panini:

Ingredients:

- 2 slices whole wheat bread
- 2 oz. sliced turkey breast
- 1 oz. sliced brie cheese
- 1/2 apple, thinly sliced
- 1 tablespoon whole-grain mustard
- 1 tablespoon honey
- 1 tablespoon olive oil

Instructions:

1. Put a sandwich press or a skillet on medium heat to warm up.
2. On one side of each slice of bread, spread whole-grain mustard and honey.
3. Put small pieces of turkey breast, brie cheese, and apple on one slice of bread.
4. Place the other slice of bread on top, with the honey-mustard side facing in.
5. Olive oil should be spread on both pieces of bread.
6. Use the panini press or a saucepan to grill the sandwich until the bread is crisp and the cheese is melted.
7. Half the sandwich and serve it hot.

Spinach And Feta Cheese Tart:

Ingredients:

- 1 pie crust
- 2 cups fresh spinach leaves
- 1/2 cup crumbled feta cheese
- 2 eggs
- 1/2 cup milk
- Salt and pepper to taste
- 1 tablespoon olive oil

Instructions:

1. Set oven temperature to 375°F (190°C).
2. Roll out the pie crust and put it in a tart pan that's 9 inches in diameter.
3. Cook fresh spinach leaves in olive oil in a pan until they are soft.
4. On the bottom of the pie crust, sprinkle chopped feta cheese.
5. Cooked spinach goes on top of the cheese.
6. Whisk together eggs, milk, salt, and pepper in a bowl.
7. Pour the egg mixture on top of the cheese and spinach.
8. Bake the tart in the oven for 25 to 30 minutes or until the filling is set and the shell is golden brown.
9. Please wait a few minutes before cutting the pie and serving it.

Warm Beet And Goat Cheese Salad:

Ingredients:

- 2 beets, cooked and sliced
- 2 cups mixed greens
- 1/4 cup crumbled goat cheese
- 2 tablespoons chopped fresh herbs (such as parsley or basil)
- Salt and pepper to taste
- 1 tablespoon olive oil
- 1 tablespoon balsamic vinegar
- 1 teaspoon honey

Instructions:

1. Set oven temperature to 375°F (190°C).
2. Put the sliced cooked beets on a baking sheet.
3. Salt and pepper to taste, then drizzle olive oil over the beets.
4. Roast the beets in the oven for about 15 to 20 minutes or until they are soft and have a light caramelization.
5. Mix mixed greens, crumbled goat cheese, and finely chopped fresh herbs

in a bowl.

6. Whisk together balsamic vinegar and honey in a different bowl to make the dressing.
7. Mix the balsamic dressing with the mixed veggies and goat cheese.
8. Warm cooked beets go on top of the salad.
9. Serve right away.

Smoked Salmon And Cream Cheese Sushi Rolls:

Ingredients:

- 2 sheets of sushi nori
- 1 cup cooked sushi rice
- 4 oz. smoked salmon, sliced
- 2 oz. cream cheese softened
- 1/2 cucumber, julienned
- 1/2 avocado, sliced
- Soy sauce for dipping

Instructions:

1. Put a sheet of sushi nori on a sushi mat or a clean kitchen towel.
2. Spread cooked sushi rice over the nori, leaving a 1-inch line at the top.
3. Spread cream cheese that has been softened over the rice.
4. Put slices of smoked salmon, cucumber strips, and avocado slices on the cream cheese.
5. Use the sushi mat or a towel to help you tighten the sushi.
6. Repeat with the last sheet of nori and the rest of the ingredients.
7. Cut each sushi roll into 6–8 pieces with a sharp knife.
8. Serve with soy sauce on the side to dip.

Grilled Vegetable And Mozzarella Sandwich:

Ingredients:

- 2 slices whole wheat bread
- 1/2 zucchini, sliced
- 1/2 red bell pepper, sliced
- 1/2 onion, sliced
- 2 oz. fresh mozzarella cheese, sliced
- Salt and pepper to taste
- 1 tablespoon olive oil

Instructions:

1. Set a grill or grill pan to medium-high heat to get it ready.
2. Olive oil was brushed on slices of zucchini, red bell pepper, and onion.
3. Salt and pepper can be added to taste.
4. About 3–4 minutes per side until the veggies are soft and have a light char.
5. Put the veggies that you grilled on a slice of whole wheat bread.
6. Sliced fresh mozzarella cheese goes on top.
7. Put the other bread slice on top.
8. Use a panini press or a saucepan to grill the sandwich until the bread is crispy and the cheese is melted.
9. The sandwich should be cut in half and served hot.

Chicken And Vegetable Rice Bowl:

Ingredients:

- 1 cup brown rice
- 2 cups chicken broth
- 2 boneless, skinless chicken breasts, diced
- 1 red bell pepper, diced
- 1 yellow bell pepper, diced
- 1 small onion, diced
- 2 cloves garlic, minced
- 2 tablespoons olive oil
- Salt and pepper, to taste

Instructions:

1. Rinse the rice well, then put it in a pot with chicken broth. Bring to a boil, then turn down the heat and let it simmer for about 45 minutes or until the rice is done.
2. At the same time, heat the olive oil in a big skillet over medium-high heat. Add the chicken pieces and cook for another 5 to 7 minutes or until the chicken is done.
3. Dice some bell peppers, onion, and garlic and add them to the chicken in the pan. Add salt and pepper, and cook for another 5 to 7 minutes, until the veggies are soft.
4. When the rice is done, split it between four bowls. Chicken and vegetables will go on top.
5. Serve right away, and have fun!

Zucchini And Corn Fritters:

Ingredients:

- 1 large zucchini, grated
- 1 can of corn kernels, drained
- 1/4 cup all-purpose flour
- 1/4 cup grated Parmesan cheese
- 1 egg, beaten
- 2 tablespoons olive oil
- Salt and pepper, to taste

Instructions:

1. Mix grated zucchini, corn kernels, flour, Parmesan cheese, and an egg beaten in a big bowl. Mix everything well until it's all mixed.
2. In a big pan over medium-high heat, heat the olive oil.
3. Use a spoon or your hands to shape the zucchini and corn into small burgers.
4. Put the patties in the pan and cook for about 3–4 minutes until golden brown and crispy.
5. Put the cakes out of the pan on a plate lined with paper towels to cool.
6. Salt and pepper the patties to your taste.
7. Serve right away, and have fun!

Spicy Tofu And Vegetable Lettuce Wraps:

Ingredients:

- 1 block firm tofu, drained and diced
- 1 red bell pepper, diced
- 1 yellow bell pepper, diced
- 1 small onion, diced
- 2 cloves garlic, minced
- 2 tablespoons soy sauce
- 1 tablespoon sriracha sauce

- 1 tablespoon honey
- 1 tablespoon sesame oil
- Salt and pepper, to taste
- 8-10 large lettuce leaves, rinsed and dried

Instructions:

1. Over medium-high heat, heat the sesame oil in a large pan. Add diced tofu and cook for 5 to 7 minutes or until lightly browned.
2. Dice bell peppers, onion, and garlic and add them to the tofu in the pan. Add salt and pepper, and cook for another 5 to 7 minutes, until the veggies are soft.
3. Whisk the soy sauce, sriracha sauce, and honey in a small bowl.
4. Add the sauce to the tofu and veggies already in the pan. Stir everything together well, and cook for another 1–2 minutes.
5. Pour the tofu and veggie mixture into lettuce leaves and roll them up to serve.
6. Serve right away, and have fun!

Cauliflower Fried Rice With Shrimp:

Ingredients:

- 1 head cauliflower, riced
- 1 pound medium shrimp, peeled and deveined
- 1 cup frozen peas and carrots, thawed
- 1 small onion, diced
- 2 cloves garlic, minced
- 2 tablespoons soy sauce
- 1 tablespoon sesame oil
- 1 tablespoon olive oil
- 2 eggs, beaten
- Salt and pepper, to taste
- Optional: sliced green onions and sesame seeds for garnish

Instructions:

1. Olive oil is heated over medium-high heat in a large pot. Add the chopped onion and garlic and cook for about two to three minutes, until the onion is transparent.
2. Put shrimp in the pan and cook it until it turns pink and is done. Take the shrimp out of the pan and set them away.
3. Add riced cauliflower to the same pan and cook for 5–7 minutes or until soft.
4. Mix peas and carrots with the cauliflower in the pan. Mix everything and cook for another 2–3 minutes.
5. Move the veggies to one side of the pan and pour the eggs on the other. Scramble the eggs until they are completely done, and then add them to the broccoli and vegetables.
6. Soy sauce and olive oil should be mixed well to the pan.
7. Add the cooked shrimp to the pan and stir well to mix everything.
8. Salt and pepper the dish to your taste.
9. Green onions and sesame seeds can be used as a garnish.
10. Serve right away, and have fun!

Lentil And Spinach Curry With Brown Rice:

Ingredients:

- 1 cup brown rice
- 2 cups vegetable broth
- 1 cup dried lentils, rinsed and drained
- 1 small onion, diced
- 2 cloves garlic, minced
- 1 tablespoon curry powder
- 1 teaspoon cumin
- 1/2 teaspoon turmeric

- 1/2 teaspoon paprika
- 1 can dice tomatoes, drained
- 2 cups fresh spinach
- Salt and pepper, to taste

Instructions:

1. Rinse the rice well, then put it in a pot with some veggie broth. Bring to a boil, then turn down the heat and let it simmer for about 45 minutes or until the rice is done.
2. Olive oil is heated over medium-high heat in a large pot. Add the chopped onion and garlic and cook for about two to three minutes, until the onion is transparent.
3. Mix in the lentils that have been cleaned, curry powder, cumin, turmeric, and paprika. Stir to mix, and let it cook for about two to three minutes.
4. Add diced tomatoes to the pan and stir well to mix everything. Simmer the mixture for 20 to 25 minutes or until the lentils are soft and cooked.
5. Add fresh spinach to the pan and mix it in well. Cook the spinach for 2 to 3 minutes or until it is soft.
6. Salt and pepper the curry to your taste.
7. When the rice is done, split it between four bowls. The bean and spinach curry goes on top.
8. Serve right away, and have fun!

Grilled Chicken And Strawberry Salad:

Ingredients:

- 1 pound boneless, skinless chicken breasts
- 1/4 cup olive oil
- 1/4 cup balsamic vinegar
- 2 tablespoons honey
- 1 teaspoon Dijon mustard
- Salt and pepper, to taste
- 6 cups mixed greens

- 1 pint fresh strawberries, hulled and sliced
- 1/4 cup sliced almonds

Instructions:
1. Set the heat on the grill to medium-high.
2. Whisk together the olive oil, balsamic vinegar, honey, and Dijon mustard in a small bowl.
3. Salt and pepper on both sides of the chicken breasts.
4. Brush the olive oil mixture on the chicken breasts.
5. Put the chicken breasts on a hot grill and cook them on each side for 5 to 7 minutes.
6. Take the chicken off the grill and sit still for about 5 minutes. The chicken should be cut into pieces.
7. Mix mixed greens, sliced strawberries, and slivered almonds in a big bowl.
8. Slice the chicken and add it to the bowl. Mix everything.
9. Pour the rest of the olive oil blend over the salad and toss it once more.
10. Salt and pepper the salad to your taste.
11. Serve right away, and have fun!

Roasted Vegetable And Feta Quinoa Bowl:

Ingredients:

- 1 cup quinoa
- 2 cups vegetable broth
- 1 red bell pepper, diced
- 1 yellow bell pepper, diced
- 1 small eggplant, diced
- 1 small onion, diced
- 2 cloves garlic, minced
- 2 tablespoons olive oil
- Salt and pepper, to taste
- 1/2 cup crumbled feta cheese
- Optional: fresh herbs, such as parsley or basil, for garnish

Instructions:

1. Rinse the quinoa well, then put it in a pot with some veggie broth. Bring to a boil, then turn down the heat and simmer for about 20 minutes or until the quinoa is fully cooked.
2. In the meantime, heat the oven to 400°F.
3. Mix diced bell peppers, eggplant, onion, and minced garlic in a big bowl. Pour olive oil over the veggies and toss well to coat.
4. Put the veggies in a single layer on a baking sheet and season with salt and pepper.
5. For about 25 to 30 minutes, or until soft and lightly browned, roast the veggies in the oven.
6. When the quinoa is done, split it between four bowls.
7. Put the roasted veggies and feta cheese on top of the quinoa.
8. Fresh herbs, like parsley or basil, can be used as a garnish.
9. Serve right away, and have fun!

Vegetarian Stuffed Tomato With Couscous:

Ingredients:

- 4 large beefsteak tomatoes
- 1 cup couscous
- 2 cups vegetable broth
- 1 small onion, diced
- 2 cloves garlic, minced
- 1 small zucchini, diced
- 1 small yellow squash, diced
- 2 tablespoons olive oil
- 1/4 cup grated Parmesan cheese
- Salt and pepper, to taste

Instructions:

1. Turn oven on to 375°F.

2. Cut the tomato tops off and use a spoon to remove the seeds and meat. Save the tomato tops and heart for something else, like making soup or tomato sauce.
3. Bring vegetable soup to a boil in a pot. Add the couscous and mix it in well. Cover the pot and take it off the stove. Let the couscous sit for about 5 minutes or until it is fully cooked.
4. Olive oil is heated over medium-high heat in a large pot. Add the chopped onion and garlic and cook for about two to three minutes, until the onion is transparent.
5. Add cut-up zucchini and yellow squash to the onion and garlic in the pan. Add salt and pepper, and cook for another 5 to 7 minutes, until the veggies are soft.
6. Cooked couscous and cooked veggies should be mixed in a large bowl. Grate some Parmesan cheese and mix it well.
7. Stuff the couscous and veggie mixture into each tomato.
8. Put the stuffed tomatoes in a baking dish and bake them for about 25 to 30 minutes or until soft and lightly browned.
9. Serve right away, and have fun!

Butternut Squash And Chickpea Salad:

Ingredients:

- 1 small butternut squash, peeled, seeded, and diced
- 1 can chickpeas, drained and rinsed
- 2 cups mixed greens
- 1/4 cup chopped walnuts
- 1/4 cup crumbled feta cheese
- 2 tablespoons olive oil
- 1 tablespoon honey
- 1 tablespoon apple cider vinegar
- Salt and pepper, to taste

Instructions:

1. Turn oven on to 400°F.
2. Mix cubed butternut squash, olive oil, honey, apple cider vinegar, salt, and pepper in a mixing bowl. Mix well to cover.
3. Spread the squash out in a single layer on a baking sheet. Roast in an oven that has already been hot for about 25 to 30 minutes or until the meat is soft and lightly browned.
4. Mix the mixed greens, roasted butternut squash, chickpeas, chopped walnuts, and crumbled feta cheese in a big bowl.
5. Pour some olive oil over the salad and mix it all up.
6. Salt and pepper the salad to your taste.
7. Serve right away, and have fun!

Chilled Avocado And Cucumber Soup:

Ingredients:
- 2 ripe avocados, peeled and pitted
- 1 large cucumber, peeled and chopped
- 2 cups vegetable broth
- 1/2 cup plain Greek yogurt
- 2 cloves garlic, minced
- 1/4 cup chopped fresh cilantro
- 2 tablespoons lime juice
- Salt and pepper, to taste

Instructions:
1. Put peeled and pitted avocados, chopped cucumber, veggie broth, plain Greek yogurt, minced garlic, chopped cilantro, lime juice, salt, and pepper in a blender or food processor and blend until smooth.
2. Mix everything until it is creamy and smooth.
3. Put the soup in the fridge for at least half an hour or until it is cold.
4. Once the soup has cooled, put it into four bowls to serve.

5. You can decorate with more chopped cilantro and a lime wedge.
6. Serve right away, and have fun!

Turkey And Pesto Pinwheels:

Ingredients:

- 1 large flour tortilla
- 2 tablespoons basil pesto
- 4-5 slices of turkey breast
- 1/4 cup shredded mozzarella cheese
- 1/4 cup chopped fresh spinach leaves

Instructions:

1. Put the flattened flour tortilla on a cutting board.
2. Spread the basil pesto over the whole tortilla equally.
3. Stack the slices of turkey breast on top of the pesto.
4. Shred some mozzarella cheese, chop some spinach leaves, and sprinkle them on top of the turkey.
5. Roll the tortilla into a pinwheel form as tightly as you can.
6. Cut the pinwheel into pieces that are 1 inch wide.
7. Serve right away, and have fun!

Vietnamese Rice Noodle Salad:

Ingredients:

- 8 oz. rice noodles
- 1 small carrot, julienned
- 1 small cucumber, julienned
- 1/4 cup chopped fresh cilantro
- 1/4 cup chopped fresh mint leaves
- 1/4 cup chopped peanuts
- 1/4 cup chopped scallions
- 2 tablespoons fish sauce
- 2 tablespoons lime juice
- 1 tablespoon honey
- 1 clove garlic, minced
- 1 small chili pepper, minced
- Salt and pepper, to taste

Instructions:

1. Follow the directions on the package to cook the rice noodles. Rinse well with cold water and let dry well.
2. Mix cooked rice noodles, julienned carrots and cucumbers, chopped cilantro, chopped mint leaves, chopped peanuts, and chopped scallions in a big bowl.
3. Mix fish sauce, lime juice, honey, minced garlic, chopped chili pepper, salt, and pepper in a small bowl with a whisk.
4. Pour the sauce over the noodle salad and toss until everything is mixed.
5. Put the noodle salad in the fridge for at least 30 minutes or until it is cold.
6. You can eat the noodle salad cold.

Eggplant Parmesan Sandwich:

Ingredients:

- 1 large eggplant, sliced into 1/4-inch rounds
- 1/2 cup all-purpose flour
- 2 eggs, beaten
- 1 cup seasoned breadcrumbs
- 1 cup marinara sauce
- 4 slices of provolone cheese
- 4 hoagie rolls, split
- 2 tablespoons olive oil
- Salt and pepper, to taste
- Optional: fresh basil leaves for garnish

Instructions:

1. Turn oven on to 400°F.
2. Salt and pepper on both sides of the eggplant pieces.
3. Plain flour should be put in a small dish. Beat eggs in another small dish. In a third small dish, put breadcrumbs that have been spiced.
4. Dip each slice of eggplant in flour, egg, and breadcrumbs, and coat both sides.
5. Put the slices of fried eggplant in a single layer on a baking sheet.
6. Drizzle the eggplant slices with olive oil and bake them for about 15 to 20 minutes or until golden brown and crispy.
7. Take the slices out of the oven and set them away.
8. Put the cut side up of the hoagie rolls on a baking sheet. Put a slice of provolone cheese on the bottom half of each roll.
9. A few drops of marinara sauce go on top of the provolone cheese.
10. On top of the tomato sauce, put a few slices of baked eggplant.
11. Add another slice of provolone cheese on top of the eggplant.

12. Put the baking sheet with the hoagie rolls back in the oven and bake for 5–10 minutes or until the cheese is melted and bubbly.
13. Take the sandwiches out of the oven and give them a few minutes to cool down.
14. Fresh basil leaves can be used as a garnish if you want.
15. Serve right away, and have fun!

Roasted Vegetable And Goat Cheese Frittata:

Ingredients:

- 6 large eggs
- 1/2 cup crumbled goat cheese
- 1 red bell pepper, diced
- 1 small onion, diced
- 1 small zucchini, diced
- 2 cloves garlic, minced
- 2 tablespoons olive oil
- Salt and pepper, to taste

Instructions:

1. Turn oven on to 375°F.
2. In a big bowl, beat eggs until they get foamy.
3. Stir the chopped goat cheese into the beaten eggs well.
4. Olive oil should be heated over medium-high heat in a big oven-safe skillet. Add the chopped onion and garlic and cook for about two to three minutes, until the onion is transparent.
5. Add diced red bell pepper and zucchini to the pan with the onion and garlic. Add salt and pepper, and cook for another 5 to 7 minutes, until the veggies are soft.
6. Place the skillet in a preheated oven and bake for 10 to 15 minutes or until the veggies are lightly browned and soft.

7. Pour the egg and goat cheese mixture over the veggies in the skillet.
8. Slowly stir the mixture using a spatula so that the vegetables and cheese are spread out evenly in the skillet.
9. Place the pan in the oven and bake for 20 to 25 minutes, or until the top of the frittata is lightly browned, and the eggs are done.
10. Take the pan out of the oven and cool down for a few minutes.
11. Remove the sides of the frittata from the pan with a spatula.
12. You can serve the frittata hot or at room temperature by cutting it into wedges.

Caponata With Whole Wheat Crostini:

Ingredients for Caponata:

- 1 large eggplant, diced
- 1 small onion, diced
- 2 cloves garlic, minced
- 1 can diced tomatoes
- 1/4 cup chopped green olives
- 1/4 cup chopped raisins
- 2 tablespoons capers
- 2 tablespoons red wine vinegar
- 2 tablespoons olive oil
- Salt and pepper, to taste

Ingredients for Whole Wheat Crostini:

- 1 small whole wheat baguette, sliced into rounds
- 2 tablespoons olive oil
- Salt and pepper, to taste

Instructions:
1. Turn oven on to 400°F.
2. Olive oil is heated over medium-high heat in a large pot. Add the chopped onion and garlic and cook for about two to three minutes, until the onion is transparent.
3. Add the diced eggplant to the onion and garlic in the pan. Add salt and pepper, and cook for another 8 to 10 minutes, until the eggplant is soft and lightly browned.
4. Mix the eggplant with diced tomatoes, chopped green olives, raisins, capers, and vinegar.
5. Cook the ingredients for 5–7 minutes or until warm and well-mixed.
6. While that happens, put the rounds of sliced whole wheat bread on a baking sheet. Salt and pepper the bread and drizzle it with olive oil.

7. Toast the bread for about 5–7 minutes in an oven that has already been hot.
8. Serve the caponata, hot or at room temperature, and the whole wheat toast.

Asparagus, Pea, And Feta Pasta Salad:

Ingredients:

- 8 oz. whole wheat fusilli pasta
- 1 lb. asparagus, trimmed and cut into 1-inch pieces
- 1 cup frozen peas, thawed
- 1/2 cup crumbled feta cheese
- 1/4 cup chopped fresh mint leaves
- 2 tablespoons olive oil
- 2 tablespoons lemon juice
- 1 clove garlic, minced
- Salt and pepper, to taste

Instructions:

1. Follow the directions on the package to cook the pasta. Rinse well with cold water and let dry well.
2. Blanch asparagus in a pot of hot, salted water for about 3 to 4 minutes or until it is soft but still has a little crunch. To stop the cooking process, drain and rinse under cold water.
3. Mix cooked pasta, blanched asparagus, thawed peas, crumbled feta cheese, and chopped mint leaves in a big bowl.
4. Whisk together the olive oil, lemon juice, chopped garlic, salt, and pepper in a small bowl.
5. Pour the dressing over the pasta salad and toss it until everything is well-mixed.
6. Put the pasta salad in the fridge for at least 30 minutes or until it is cold.
7. Cold pasta salad is delicious.

Carrot And Ginger Soup With Whole Wheat Bread:

Ingredients for Soup:

- 1 pound carrots, peeled and chopped
- 1 small onion, chopped
- 2 cloves garlic, minced
- 1 tablespoon grated ginger
- 4 cups vegetable broth
- 1/2 cup plain Greek yogurt
- 2 tablespoons olive oil
- Salt and pepper, to taste

Ingredients for Whole Wheat Bread:

- 1 small whole wheat baguette, sliced
- 2 tablespoons olive oil
- Salt and pepper, to taste

Instructions:

1. Olive oil is heated in a big pot over medium-high heat. Add the chopped onion and garlic and cook for about two to three minutes, until the onion is transparent.
2. Add chopped carrots and grated ginger to the pot along with the onion and garlic. Salt and pepper the carrots, then cook for 5 to 7 minutes or until soft.
3. Put some vegetable stock in the pot and bring it to a boil.
4. Turn down the heat and let the soup cook for 20 to 25 minutes or until the carrots are very soft.
5. You can use an immersion mixer or put the soup in a blender or food processor and blend it until it is smooth and creamy.
6. Whisk the soup with the Greek yogurt until everything is well-mixed.
7. While that happens, put the rounds of sliced whole wheat bread on a baking sheet. Salt and pepper the bread and drizzle it with olive oil.

8. Bake the bread in a warm oven at 375°F for about 5 to 7 minutes or until it is lightly toasted.
9. Hot whole wheat bread should be served with carrot and ginger soup.

Grilled Halloumi And Watermelon Salad:

Ingredients:

- 1/2 small seedless watermelon, cut into cubes
- 8 oz. halloumi cheese, cut into slices
- 1/4 cup chopped fresh mint leaves
- 1/4 cup chopped fresh parsley
- 2 tablespoons olive oil
- 2 tablespoons balsamic vinegar
- Salt and pepper, to taste

Instructions:
1. Set the heat on the grill to medium-high.
2. Mix cubed watermelon, chopped mint leaves, and chopped parsley

in a big bowl.

3. Whisk together the olive oil, balsamic vinegar, salt, and pepper in a small bowl.
4. Pour the dressing over the fruit mixture and toss until everything is mixed well.
5. Grill the halloumi slices for 1–2 minutes per side or until they are lightly browned and hot.
6. Place the halloumi pieces grilled on top of the watermelon salad.
7. Serve the salad right away, and have fun!

Mediterranean Chickpea Salad:

Ingredients:

- 2 cans chickpeas, drained and rinsed
- 1 small red onion, chopped
- 1 small red bell pepper, chopped
- 1 small cucumber, chopped
- 1/4 cup chopped fresh parsley
- 1/4 cup chopped fresh mint
- 2 tablespoons olive oil
- 2 tablespoons lemon juice
- 1 clove garlic, minced
- Salt and pepper, to taste
- Optional: crumbled feta cheese

Instructions:

1. Mix the drained and rinsed chickpeas, chopped red onion, chopped red bell pepper, and chopped cucumber in a big bowl.
2. Add fresh chopped parsley and freshly chopped mint to the bowl.
3. Whisk together the olive oil, lemon juice, chopped garlic, salt, and pepper in a small bowl.
4. Pour the sauce over the chickpea salad and toss until everything is mixed.
5. Crumbled feta cheese can be added on top if you want.
6. Put the chickpea salad in the fridge for at least 30 minutes or until it is cold.
7. Enjoy the chickpea salad when it's cold.

Nicoise Salad With Grilled Tuna:

Ingredients:

- 2 6-oz. tuna steaks
- 1 lb. baby potatoes, boiled until tender
- 4 hard-boiled eggs, sliced
- 1 cup cherry tomatoes, halved

- 1/2 small red onion, sliced
- 1/2 cup sliced black olives
- 1/4 cup chopped fresh parsley
- 2 tablespoons Dijon mustard
- 2 tablespoons red wine vinegar
- 1/2 cup olive oil
- Salt and pepper, to taste

Instructions:
1. Set the heat on the grill to medium-high.
2. Add salt and pepper to the tuna steaks.
3. Grill the tuna steaks for 2 to 3 minutes on each side or until they are as done as you like them.
4. Put boiled baby potatoes, sliced hard-boiled eggs, halved cherry tomatoes, sliced red onion, sliced black olives, and chopped fresh parsley into a large mixing bowl.
5. Whisk together Dijon mustard, red wine vinegar, olive oil, salt, and pepper in a small bowl.
6. Pour the dressing over the salad and toss everything together until everything is well-mixed.
7. Put the tuna steaks that have been cooked on top of the salad.
8. Serve the salad right away, and have fun!

Cold Soba Noodle Salad With Vegetables:

Ingredients:
- 8 oz. soba noodles
- 1 red bell pepper, julienned
- 1 small carrot, julienned
- 1 small cucumber, julienned
- 1/4 cup chopped scallions
- 1/4 cup chopped cilantro
- 2 tablespoons sesame oil
- 2 tablespoons rice vinegar

- 1 tablespoon honey
- 1 tablespoon soy sauce
- 1 teaspoon grated ginger
- Salt and pepper, to taste

Instructions:
1. Follow the directions on the package to cook soba noodles. Rinse well with cold water and let dry well.
2. Mix cooked soba noodles, red bell pepper strips, carrot strips, cucumber strips, chopped scallions, and chopped cilantro in a big bowl.
3. Whisk together sesame oil, rice vinegar, honey, soy sauce, chopped ginger, salt, and pepper in a small mixing bowl.
4. Pour the sauce over the noodle salad and toss until everything is mixed.
5. Put the noodle salad in the fridge for at least 30 minutes or until it is cold.
6. You can eat the noodle salad cold.

Roasted Brussels Sprout And Quinoa Salad:

Ingredients:
- 1 lb. Brussels sprouts, trimmed and halved
- 1 cup cooked quinoa
- 1/2 cup dried cranberries
- 1/2 cup chopped walnuts
- 1/4 cup chopped fresh parsley
- 2 tablespoons olive oil
- 2 tablespoons balsamic vinegar
- 1 tablespoon honey
- Salt and pepper, to taste

Instructions:
1. Turn oven on to 400°F.
2. Mix halved Brussels sprouts, olive oil, salt, and pepper in a big bowl.

3. Place the Brussels sprouts on a baking sheet and roast them in the oven for about 20 to 25 minutes or until they are lightly browned and soft.
4. Mix together cooked quinoa, dried cranberries, chopped walnuts, and chopped fresh parsley in a big bowl.
5. Mix the balsamic vinegar, honey, salt, and pepper in a small bowl with a whisk.
6. Pour the dressing over the quinoa salad and toss until everything is mixed.
7. After cooking the Brussels sprouts, add them to the quinoa salad.
8. Serve the salad at room temperature or warm, and enjoy!

Rainbow Veggie And Hummus Wrap:

Ingredients:
- 1 large whole wheat tortilla wrap
- 1/2 cup hummus
- 1/2 small red bell pepper, thinly sliced
- 1/2 small yellow bell pepper, thinly sliced
- 1/2 small green bell pepper, thinly sliced
- 1 small carrot, peeled and thinly sliced
- 1/2 small cucumber, thinly sliced
- 1/4 cup crumbled feta cheese
- Salt and pepper, to taste

Instructions:
1. Spread the hummus on the wrap made of whole wheat tortillas.
2. On top of the hummus, layer the thinly sliced red, yellow, and green bell peppers, carrot, and onion.
3. Salt and pepper to taste, then sprinkle chopped feta cheese over the vegetables.
4. Tightly roll up the wrap and cut it in half.
5. Serve the wrap and have some fun!

Black Bean And Mango Salad With Lime Dressing:

Ingredients:

- 2 cups cooked black beans, drained and rinsed
- 1 large mango, peeled and diced
- 1 small red onion, diced
- 1 small red bell pepper, diced
- 1/4 cup chopped fresh cilantro
- 2 tablespoons olive oil
- 2 tablespoons fresh lime juice
- 1 teaspoon honey
- Salt and pepper, to taste

Instructions:

1. Mix cooked black beans, diced mango, red onion, red bell pepper, and chopped fresh cilantro in a big bowl.
2. Whisk together olive oil, fresh lime juice, honey, salt, and pepper in a small bowl.
3. Pour the dressing over the salad and toss everything together until everything is well-mixed.
4. Put the salad in the fridge for at least 30 minutes or until it is cold.
5. Enjoy the salad when it's cold.

Lemon Herb Grilled Salmon:

Ingredients:

- 4 salmon fillets (6 oz. each)
- 2 tablespoons olive oil
- 2 tablespoons fresh lemon juice
- 2 cloves garlic, minced
- 1 tablespoon chopped fresh thyme
- 1 tablespoon chopped fresh rosemary
- Salt and pepper, to taste

Instructions:

1. Whisk together olive oil, fresh lemon juice, minced garlic, chopped fresh thyme, chopped fresh rosemary, salt, and pepper in a small mixing bowl.
2. Pour the marinade over the salmon pieces in a big dish. Marinate for 30 minutes or up to two hours.
3. Set the grill's heat to medium-high.
4. Put the pieces of salmon on the grill with the skin side down.
5. Cook the salmon on the grill for 4 to 5 minutes per side or until it's as done as you like.
6. Serve the cooked salmon while it's hot, and enjoy!

Whole Wheat Spaghetti With Marinara Sauce:

Ingredients:

- 8 oz. whole wheat spaghetti
- 1 small onion, diced
- 2 cloves garlic, minced
- 1 can diced tomatoes
- 1/4 cup chopped fresh basil

- 2 tablespoons olive oil
- Salt and pepper, to taste
- Optional: grated Parmesan cheese

Instructions:
1. Follow the directions on the package to cook whole wheat spaghetti. Rinse well with cold water and let dry well.
2. Olive oil is heated over medium-high heat in a large pot. Add the diced onion and minced garlic and cook for another two to three minutes or until the onion is transparent.
3. Mix the diced tomatoes with the onion and garlic in the pan.
4. Season with salt and pepper and cook for 10 to 15 minutes until the tomatoes break down and the sauce thickens.
5. Mix the chopped fresh basil and marinara sauce in the pan until everything is well-mixed.
6. Put the cooked whole wheat spaghetti and marinara sauce in the pan and toss until the pasta is well covered.
7. Grated Parmesan cheese can be added on top if you want.
8. Serve the whole wheat spaghetti with the tomato sauce hot, and enjoy!

Roasted Chicken With Root Vegetables:

Ingredients:

- 1 whole chicken (3-4 lbs.)
- 2 large carrots, peeled and chopped
- 2 large parsnips, peeled and chopped
- 1 small onion, chopped
- 4 cloves garlic, minced
- 2 tablespoons olive oil
- 1 tablespoon chopped fresh rosemary
- 1 tablespoon chopped fresh thyme
- Salt and pepper, to taste

Instructions:

1. Turn oven on to 375°F.
2. Cut the carrots, parsnips, and onion into small pieces and put them in a big roasting pan.
3. Sprinkle salt, pepper, chopped fresh rosemary, and chopped fresh thyme over the veggies and drizzle olive oil.
4. Put the whole chicken on top of the veggies in the roasting pan.
5. Add salt and pepper to the chicken.
6. About 1-1/2 to 2 hours, or until the chicken is fully cooked (the internal temperature should hit 165°F), roast the chicken and vegetables in an oven that has been heated.
7. Wait about 10 minutes before cutting into the chicken.
8. Serve the roasted chicken with the root veggies while they are still hot.

Vegetarian Lentil Shepherd's Pie:

Ingredients:

- 2 cups cooked green or brown lentils
- 1 large onion, chopped
- 2 cloves garlic, minced
- 2 large carrots, peeled and chopped
- 1 large parsnip, peeled and chopped
- 1 cup frozen peas
- 2 tablespoons olive oil
- 1 tablespoon chopped fresh thyme
- 1 tablespoon chopped fresh rosemary
- Salt and pepper, to taste
- 4 cups mashed potatoes
- Optional: grated Cheddar cheese

Instructions:

1. Turn oven on to 375°F.
2. Olive oil is heated over medium-high heat in a large pot. Add the chopped onion and crushed garlic and cook for 2 to 3 minutes or until the onion is transparent.
3. Mix chopped carrots and parsnips with the chopped onion and garlic in the pan. Season with salt, pepper, fresh thyme, and rosemary that I chopped up.
4. Cook the vegetables for about 10–15 minutes or until soft.
5. Mix the cooked lentils and frozen peas with the vegetables in the pan. Stir everything together until everything is mixed well.
6. Put the lentils and vegetables in a big baking dish.
7. Put the mashed potatoes on top of the lentils and vegetables.
8. Grated Cheddar cheese can be added on top if you want.
9. Shepherd's pie needs about 25 to 30 minutes to get hot and bubbly in the oven.

10. Serve the vegetarian shepherd's pie with hot lentils, and enjoy!

Black Bean And Sweet Potato Chili:

Ingredients:

- 2 tablespoons olive oil
- 1 small onion, chopped
- 2 cloves garlic, minced
- 1 large sweet potato, peeled and chopped
- 1 red bell pepper, chopped
- 1 green bell pepper, chopped
- 1 can black beans, drained and rinsed
- 1 can diced tomatoes
- 2 cups vegetable broth
- 2 teaspoons chili powder
- 1 teaspoon ground cumin
- Salt and pepper, to taste

Instructions:

1. Olive oil is heated in a big pot over medium-high heat. Add the chopped onion and crushed garlic and cook for 2 to 3 minutes or until the onion is transparent.
2. Add chopped onion, garlic, sweet potato, red bell pepper, and green bell pepper to the pot.
3. Add salt, pepper, chili powder, and ground cumin.
4. Put diced tomatoes, black beans, and veggie broth in the pot.
5. Bring the chili to a boil and cook for about 20 to 25 minutes until the sweet potato is soft and the flavors have mixed well.
6. Serve the sweet potato and black bean soup hot, and enjoy!

Chicken And Vegetable Stir-Fry With Brown Rice:

Ingredients:

- 1 lb. boneless, skinless chicken breasts cut into thin strips
- 2 cups mixed vegetables (such as broccoli, carrots, snow peas, bell peppers, etc.), cut into bite-sized pieces
- 1 small onion, chopped
- 2 cloves garlic, minced
- 2 tablespoons olive oil
- 1 tablespoon soy sauce
- 1 tablespoon hoisin sauce
- 1 tablespoon honey
- 2 cups cooked brown rice
- Salt and pepper, to taste

Instructions:

1. Heat the olive oil over medium-high heat in a big pan or wok. Add the chopped onion and crushed garlic and cook for 2 to 3 minutes or until the onion is transparent.
2. Add chicken strips to the pan and cook for about 5 to 7 minutes or until the chicken is no longer pink.
3. Stir-fry the mixed veggies for about three to five minutes or until they are crisp-tender.
4. Whisk together the soy sauce, hoisin sauce, honey, salt, and pepper in a small bowl.
5. Pour the sauce over the stir-fry and toss it together until everything is well-mixed.
6. Serve the stir-fried chicken and veggies with cooked brown rice, and enjoy!

Seared Scallops With Asparagus:

Ingredients:

- 1 lb. large sea scallops, rinsed and patted dry
- 1 lb. asparagus, trimmed
- 2 cloves garlic, minced
- 2 tablespoons olive oil
- 1 tablespoon butter
- Salt and pepper, to taste
- Lemon wedges for serving

Instructions:

1. Add salt and pepper to both sides of the sea scallops.
2. In a big pan over medium-high heat, heat the olive oil. Add chopped garlic and cook for about 30 seconds or until the garlic smells good.
3. Add the scallops seasoned to the pan and cook for about two to three minutes on each side or until golden brown and toasted.
4. Take the scallops out of the pan and place them on a plate.
5. Add the clipped asparagus to the same pan and cook for about 5 to 7 minutes, or until the asparagus is tender but still slightly crunchy.
6. Add butter to the pan and stir until the butter has melted and the asparagus is well mixed.
7. Serve the scallops grilled with cooked asparagus and wedges of lemon.
8. Enjoy your delicious meal!

Eggplant And Chickpea Curry:

Ingredients:

- 1 large eggplant, chopped
- 1 can chickpeas, drained and rinsed
- 1 large onion, chopped
- 2 cloves garlic, minced
- 2 tablespoons olive oil
- 2 tablespoons curry powder
- 1 can diced tomatoes
- 1 can of coconut milk
- Salt and pepper, to taste
- Chopped fresh cilantro for serving

Instructions:

1. Olive oil is heated over medium-high heat in a large pot. Add the chopped onion and crushed garlic and cook for 2 to 3 minutes or until the onion is transparent.
2. Chop up some eggplant and add it to the pan. Stir it around until the oil and onions cover the eggplant.
3. Add curry powder, salt, and pepper to taste.
4. Add beans rinsed and drained to the pan with the eggplant and onion.
5. Dice some tomatoes and pour some coconut milk into the pan.
6. Stir everything together until everything is mixed well.
7. Bring the curry to a boil and cook for 15–20 minutes, until the eggplant is soft and the flavors have mixed well.
8. Serve the soup with hot eggplant and chickpeas, with chopped fresh cilantro.
9. Enjoy your delicious meal!

Mediterranean Stuffed Chicken Breast:

Ingredients:

- 4 boneless, skinless chicken breasts
- 1/2 cup crumbled feta cheese
- 1/4 cup chopped sun-dried tomatoes
- 1/4 cup chopped kalamata olives
- 2 cloves garlic, minced
- 2 tablespoons chopped fresh parsley
- 2 tablespoons olive oil
- Salt and pepper, to taste

Instructions:

1. Turn oven on to 375°F.
2. Mix crumbled feta cheese, chopped sun-dried tomatoes, chopped kalamata olives, minced garlic, and chopped fresh parsley in a small mixing bowl.
3. Cut a hole in each chicken breast with a sharp knife. Be careful to cut only some of the way through.
4. Fill each chicken breast hole with the feta mixture.
5. Salt and pepper on both sides of the chicken breasts that have been stuffed.
6. In a big pan over medium-high heat, heat the olive oil.
7. Add the stuffed chicken breasts to the pan and cook for about two to three minutes on each side or until golden brown and toasted.
8. Place the chicken breasts that have been browned in a baking dish.
9. Bake the stuffed chicken breasts in an oven that has already been warm for 20 to 25 minutes or until they are no longer pink in the middle.
10. Serve the stuffed chicken breasts from the Mediterranean hot, and enjoy!

Shrimp And Vegetable Skewers:

Ingredients:

- 1 lb. large shrimp, peeled and deveined
- 2 bell peppers, cut into bite-sized pieces
- 1 large zucchini, cut into bite-sized pieces
- 1 large onion, cut into bite-sized pieces
- 2 tablespoons olive oil
- 2 cloves garlic, minced
- 1 tablespoon chopped fresh thyme
- Salt and pepper, to taste
- Lemon wedges for serving

Instructions:

1. Soak wooden skewers in water for at least 30 minutes before using.
2. Set the heat on the grill to medium-high.
3. Shrimp, bell peppers, zucchini, and onion should be threaded onto the skewers.
4. Whisk together olive oil, crushed garlic, chopped fresh thyme, salt, and pepper in a small mixing bowl.
5. Brush the shrimp and veggies on the skewers with the olive oil mix.
6. Grill the shrimp and vegetables on skewers for two to three minutes on each side or until the shrimp turns pink and is cooked.
7. Serve the shrimp and vegetables on skewers while they are still hot and with wedges of lemon.
8. Enjoy your delicious meal!

Spinach And Mushroom Stuffed Bell Peppers:

Ingredients:

- 4 bell peppers, tops removed and seeded
- 2 cups chopped fresh spinach
- 1 cup chopped mushrooms
- 1 small onion, chopped
- 2 cloves garlic, minced
- 1 cup cooked brown rice
- 1/2 cup shredded mozzarella cheese
- 2 tablespoons olive oil
- Salt and pepper, to taste

Instructions:

1. Turn oven on to 375°F.
2. Olive oil is heated over medium-high heat in a large pot. Add the chopped onion and crushed garlic and cook for 2 to 3 minutes or until the onion is transparent.
3. Chop up some mushrooms and add them to the onion and garlic in the pan. Cook the mushrooms for about 5–7 minutes or until soft.
4. Add chopped fresh spinach to the pan and stir everything together until the spinach has wilted.
5. Add cooked brown rice to the pan and stir everything together until everything is well-mixed.
6. Add salt and pepper to taste the mixture.
7. Stuff the spinach and mushroom mix into the bell peppers.
8. Shreds of mozzarella cheese go on top of each stuffed bell pepper.
9. Bake the stuffed bell peppers in the oven for about 25 to 30 minutes or until the cheese is melted and bubbly.
10. Serve the bell peppers stuffed with spinach and mushrooms hot, and enjoy!

Grilled Vegetable And Quinoa Salad:

Ingredients:

- 1 cup cooked quinoa
- 1 small zucchini, sliced
- 1 small yellow squash, sliced
- 1 red bell pepper, seeded and sliced
- 1 orange bell pepper, seeded and sliced
- 1 small red onion, sliced
- 2 tablespoons olive oil
- Salt and pepper, to taste
- 2 tablespoons balsamic vinegar
- 1 tablespoon chopped fresh basil
- 1 tablespoon chopped fresh parsley

Instructions:

1. Set the heat on the grill to medium-high.
2. Sliced zucchini, yellow squash, red bell pepper, orange bell pepper, and red onion are mixed with olive oil, salt, and pepper in a big mixing bowl.
3. Grill the vegetables for 5–7 minutes on each side or until they are soft and have a little bit of a char.
4. Whisk together balsamic vinegar, chopped fresh basil, and chopped fresh parsley
5. in a small mixing bowl.
6. Mix cooked quinoa, grilled vegetables, and balsamic vinaigrette in a big bowl.
7. The grilled vegetable and rice salad can be served at room temperature or cold.
8. Enjoy your delicious meal!

Baked Cod With Cherry Tomatoes And Olives:

Ingredients:

- 4 cod fillets
- 1-pint cherry tomatoes
- 1/2 cup kalamata olives, pitted
- 2 cloves garlic, minced
- 2 tablespoons olive oil
- Salt and pepper, to taste
- 1 tablespoon chopped fresh parsley
- Lemon wedges for serving

Instructions:

1. Turn oven on to 375°F.
2. Mix minced garlic, olive oil, and pitted kalamata olives with cherry tomatoes and kalamata olives in a big bowl.
3. Add salt and pepper to taste the mixture.
4. Put the cod pieces in a dish for baking.
5. Pour the mixture of cherry tomatoes and olives over the pieces of cod.
6. Bake the cod in the oven for 15 to 20 minutes or until the fish is cooked and flakes easily with a fork.
7. Sprinkle chopped fresh parsley on top of the cod pieces that have been baked.
8. Add cherry tomatoes, hot olives, and lemon wedges to the baking cod.
9. Enjoy your delicious meal!

Lentil And Vegetable Stew:

Ingredients:

- 1 cup dry green lentils, rinsed and drained
- 1 large onion, chopped
- 2 cloves garlic, minced
- 2 carrots, chopped
- 2 celery stalks, chopped
- 1 red bell pepper, chopped
- 1 can diced tomatoes
- 4 cups vegetable broth
- 1 tablespoon olive oil
- 1 tablespoon chopped fresh thyme
- Salt and pepper, to taste

Instructions:

1. Olive oil is heated in a big pot over medium-high heat. Add the chopped onion and crushed garlic and cook for 2 to 3 minutes or until the onion is transparent.
2. Add chopped carrots, celery, and red bell pepper to the pot along with the chopped onion and garlic.
3. Add salt, pepper, and chopped fresh thyme to taste.
4. Put lentils that have been rinsed and drained chopped tomatoes, and vegetable broth in the pot.
5. Bring the stew to a simmer and cook for 30–40 minutes, until the lentils and veggies are soft and the flavors have mixed well.
6. Serve the bean and vegetable stew hot, and enjoy it!

Broccoli And Cheddar Stuffed Chicken Breast:

Ingredients:

- 4 boneless, skinless chicken breasts
- 1 cup chopped broccoli florets
- 1 cup shredded cheddar cheese
- 2 cloves garlic, minced
- 2 tablespoons olive oil
- Salt and pepper, to taste
- Lemon wedges for serving

Instructions:

1. Turn oven on to 375°F.
2. Cut a hole in each chicken breast with a sharp knife. Be careful to cut only some of the way through.
3. Mix chopped broccoli pieces, shredded cheddar cheese, minced garlic, and salt and pepper to taste in a small mixing bowl.
4. Fill each chicken breast pocket with the broccoli and cheese filling.
5. Salt and pepper on both sides of the chicken breasts that have been stuffed.
6. In a big pan over medium-high heat, heat the olive oil.
7. Add the stuffed chicken breasts to the pan and cook for about two to three minutes on each side or until golden brown and toasted.
8. Place the chicken breasts that have been browned in a baking dish.
9. Bake the stuffed chicken breasts in an oven that has already been warm for 20 to 25 minutes or until they are no longer pink in the middle.
10. Serve the hot broccoli and cheddar-stuffed chicken breasts, with lemon wedges on the side.
11. Enjoy your delicious meal!

Egg Fried Brown Rice With Vegetables:

Ingredients:

- 2 cups cooked brown rice
- 1 small onion, chopped
- 2 cloves garlic, minced
- 1 small carrot, diced
- 1 small zucchini, diced
- 1 cup frozen peas
- 2 tablespoons olive oil
- 2 eggs, lightly beaten
- 2 tablespoons soy sauce
- Salt and pepper, to taste
- Chopped green onions for serving

Instructions:

1. Olive oil is heated over medium-high heat in a large pot. Add the chopped onion and crushed garlic and cook for 2 to 3 minutes or until the onion is transparent.
2. Add diced carrot, zucchini, and frozen peas to the pan along with the onion and garlic.
3. Cook the veggies for about 5–7 minutes, or until they are soft but still have some crunch.
4. Stir the cooked brown rice in with the veggies until everything is well-mixed.
5. Mix beaten eggs and soy sauce with a whisk in a small bowl.
6. Pour the egg mixture into the skillet with the rice and veggies.
7. Stir the egg mixture into the rice and veggies until the eggs are scrambled, and the rice is done.
8. Salt and pepper the fried rice to your taste.
9. Green onions cut into small pieces should be sprinkled on top of the hot egg-fried brown rice with veggies.
10. Enjoy your delicious meal!

Moroccan Chicken Tagine:

Ingredients:

- 4 chicken thighs, bone-in, skin-on
- 1 large onion, chopped
- 2 cloves garlic, minced
- 2 large carrots, peeled and chopped
- 1 red bell pepper, seeded and chopped
- 1 can chickpeas, drained and rinsed
- 1/2 cup dried apricots, chopped
- 2 tablespoons olive oil
- 1 teaspoon ground cumin
- 1 teaspoon ground coriander
- 1 teaspoon ground cinnamon
- 1 teaspoon paprika
- 1/4 teaspoon cayenne pepper
- 2 cups chicken broth
- Salt and pepper, to taste
- Chopped fresh parsley for serving

Instructions:

1. Heat the olive oil over medium-high heat in a big pot or Dutch oven. Add the chicken legs and cook them on each side for 5 to 7 minutes until they are browned.
2. Take the chicken legs out of the pot and put them somewhere else.
3. Put chopped onion, crushed garlic, carrots, and red bell pepper in the same pot.
4. Add cumin, coriander, cinnamon, paprika, cayenne pepper, paprika, salt, and pepper to taste the vegetables.
5. Stir everything together and cook for about 7 minutes or until the vegetables are soft.
6. Add chopped dried apricots and chickpeas that have been rinsed and drained to the pot.
7. Pour the chicken soup into the pot and stir it all up.
8. Return the chicken legs that have been browned to the pot.

9. Bring the tagine to a boil and cook for 30–40 minutes or until the chicken is soft.
10. Serve the chicken tagine from Morocco hot, with chopped fresh parsley.
11. Enjoy your delicious meal!

Beef And Broccoli With Brown Rice:

Ingredients:
- 1 lb. beef sirloin, sliced into thin strips
- 1 large head of broccoli, cut into small florets
- 1 small onion, chopped
- 2 cloves garlic, minced
- 2 tablespoons olive oil
- Salt and pepper, to taste
- 1/4 cup soy sauce
- 1 tablespoon honey
- 1 tablespoon cornstarch
- 2 tablespoons water
- 2 cups cooked brown rice

Instructions:
1. Olive oil is heated over medium-high heat in a large pot. Add the chopped onion and crushed garlic and cook for 2 to 3 minutes or until the onion is transparent.
2. Add the sliced beef sirloin to the pan and cook for about 5 to 7 minutes, or until all sides of the beef are cooked.
3. Add small pieces of broccoli to the beef and onion in the pan.
4. Add salt and pepper to taste to everything.
5. Whisk together the soy sauce, honey, cornstarch, and water in a small bowl.
6. Pour the soy sauce mixture over the veggies and beef in the pan.

7. Stir everything together and cook for 2 to 3 minutes, until the sauce thickens and the beef and broccoli are done.
8. Serve the beef and veggies with brown rice while it is hot, and enjoy your tasty meal.

Lemon And Herb Baked Trout:

Ingredients:
- 4 trout fillets
- 2 tablespoons olive oil
- 1 lemon, sliced
- 2 cloves garlic, minced
- 1 tablespoon chopped fresh parsley
- 1 tablespoon chopped fresh thyme
- Salt and pepper, to taste

Instructions:
1. Turn oven on to 375°F.
2. Mix the olive oil, minced garlic, chopped fresh parsley, chopped fresh thyme, salt, and pepper in a small mixing bowl.
3. Put the trout pieces in a dish for baking.
4. Brush the trout fillets with the olive oil and herb blend.
5. On top of the trout pieces, put lemon slices.
6. Bake the trout in the oven for 15 to 20 minutes or until the fish is cooked and flakes easily with a fork.
7. Serve the trout with lemon and herbs hot, and enjoy!

Spaghetti Squash With Pesto And Cherry Tomatoes:

Ingredients:

- 1 spaghetti squash, halved and seeded
- 1/4 cup pesto
- 1 pint cherry tomatoes, halved
- 2 cloves garlic, minced
- 2 tablespoons olive oil
- Salt and pepper, to taste
- Shredded Parmesan cheese for serving

Instructions:

1. Turn oven on to 375°F.
2. Salt and pepper the spaghetti squash cut in half and brushed with olive oil.
3. Cut side down, and put the spaghetti squash halves in a baking dish.
4. Bake the spaghetti squash in the oven for 30–40 minutes or until it is soft and cooked.
5. While the spaghetti squash is baking, mix cherry tomatoes cut in half, minced garlic, pesto, and salt and pepper to taste in a big bowl.
6. Please take the spaghetti squash out of the oven when it's done and let it cool for a few minutes.
7. Scrape the spaghetti squash meat into a large mixing bowl with a fork.
8. Add the tomato and pesto mixture to the spaghetti squash and stir until everything is well mixed.
9. Serve the spaghetti squash with pesto, cherry tomatoes, and Parmesan cheese on top while it is still hot.
10. Enjoy your delicious meal!

Cajun-Spiced Shrimp And Grits:

Ingredients:

- 1 lb. shrimp, peeled and deveined
- 1 cup quick-cooking grits
- 2 cups water
- 2 cups milk
- 1/2 cup shredded cheddar cheese
- 1 tablespoon butter
- 1 tablespoon olive oil
- 2 cloves garlic, minced
- 1 small onion, chopped
- 1 green bell pepper, seeded and chopped
- 1 red bell pepper, seeded and chopped
- 1 tablespoon Cajun seasoning
- Salt and pepper, to taste
- Chopped fresh parsley for serving

Instructions:

1. Bring water and milk to a boil in a big pot. Slowly whisk in grits that cook quickly, stirring all the time.
2. Turn the heat down to low and let the grits simmer, turning often, for about 5-7 minutes or until they are cooked and creamy.
3. Take the pot off the heat and stir in the cheddar cheese shreds and butter until the cheese melts and the butter is mixed.
4. Olive oil is heated over medium-high heat in a large pot. Add chopped onion, crushed garlic, green and red bell peppers, and onion.
5. Add Cajun spice, salt, and pepper to taste the vegetables.
6. For about 5–7 minutes, or until they are soft, cook the vegetables.
7. Add shrimp peeled and deveined to the pan with the vegetables.

8. Cook the shrimp for about two to three minutes on each side or until they turn pink and are done through.
9. While still hot, serve the shrimp and grits with Cajun spices and chopped fresh parsley.
10. Enjoy your delicious meal!

Vegetable And Chickpea Curry With Basmati Rice:

Ingredients:

- 1 cup basmati rice
- 2 cups water
- 1 tablespoon olive oil
- 1 small onion, chopped
- 2 cloves garlic, minced
- 1 red bell pepper, seeded and chopped
- 2 carrots, peeled and chopped
- 1 can chickpeas, drained and rinsed
- 1 can diced tomatoes
- 1/2 cup vegetable broth
- 2 tablespoons curry powder
- Salt and pepper, to taste
- Chopped fresh cilantro for serving

Instructions:

1. Run cold water through a fine-mesh sieve with the basmati rice in it.
2. Bring water to a boil in a small pot. Pour in the washed basmati rice and turn the heat down to low.
3. Cover the pot with a lid that fits tightly, and let the rice boil for 18 to 20 minutes or until it is soft.
4. Olive oil is heated over medium-high heat in a large pot. Add chopped onion, crushed garlic, carrots, and red bell pepper.

5. Cook the vegetables for about 7 to 10 minutes or until soft.
6. Add chickpeas that have been rinsed and drained, diced tomatoes from a can, veggie broth, curry powder, salt, and pepper to the pan.
7. Bring the curry to a boil and cook for 10 to 15 minutes, until the flavors have mixed well and the sauce has thickened.
8. Serve the chickpea and vegetable soup with hot basmati rice and chopped fresh cilantro on top.
9. Enjoy your delicious meal!

Oven-Baked Lemon Herb Chicken Thighs:

Ingredients:
- 4 chicken thighs, bone-in, skin-on
- 1 lemon, juiced and zested
- 2 tablespoons olive oil
- 2 cloves garlic, minced
- 1 tablespoon chopped fresh thyme
- 1 tablespoon chopped fresh rosemary
- Salt and pepper, to taste

Instructions:
1. Turn oven on to 375°F.
2. Whisk together minced garlic, chopped fresh thyme, rosemary, salt, pepper, lemon juice, and lemon zest in a small mixing bowl.
3. Put the chicken legs in a dish for baking.
4. Brush the chicken legs with the olive oil and herbs.
5. Bake the chicken legs in an oven that has already been heated for 35 to 40 minutes or until the chicken is done and the skin is crispy.
6. Serve the oven-baked chicken legs with lemon and herbs while still hot.

Mushroom Stroganoff With Whole Wheat Noodles:

Ingredients:

- 1 lb. whole wheat egg noodles
- 2 tablespoons olive oil
- 1 onion, chopped
- 2 cloves garlic, minced
- 1 lb. mushrooms, sliced
- 2 tablespoons butter
- 2 tablespoons all-purpose flour
- 1 cup beef broth
- 1/2 cup sour cream
- Salt and pepper, to taste
- Chopped fresh parsley for serving

Instructions:

1. Follow the directions on the package for cooking whole wheat egg noodles in a big pot of salted boiling water. Drain and put away.
2. Olive oil is heated over medium-high heat in a large pot. Add the chopped onion, minced garlic, and cut mushrooms.
3. Cook the vegetables for about 7 to 10 minutes or until soft.
4. In the same pan, melt butter over medium heat. Whisk in all-purpose flour until the mixture is smooth.
5. Pour the beef broth into the pan and whisk it all the time.
6. Bring the mixture to a boil and cook for 2 to 3 minutes or until the sauce thickens.
7. Add the sour cream and season to taste with salt and pepper.
8. Put the cooked whole wheat egg noodles and the mushroom stroganoff sauce in the pan.
9. Mix everything until the sauce covers the noodles well.

10. The mushroom stroganoff should be served hot with whole wheat noodles and chopped fresh parsley.
11. Enjoy your delicious meal!

Salmon And Spinach Quiche:

Ingredients:

- 1 unbaked pie crust
- 1 tablespoon olive oil
- 1 small onion, chopped
- 2 cups fresh baby spinach
- 6 oz. canned salmon, drained and flaked
- 4 large eggs
- 1 cup milk
- 1/2 cup shredded cheddar cheese
- Salt and pepper, to taste
- Chopped fresh dill for serving

Instructions:

1. Turn oven on to 375°F.
2. Put the pie crust that has yet to be baked into a 9-inch dish.
3. Olive oil is heated over medium-high heat in a large pot. Add the chopped onion and cook for about 5 minutes or until the onion is transparent.
4. Add fresh baby spinach to the pan and cook for 2 to 3 minutes, until it wilts.
5. Stir everything together after you add the canned fish to the skillet.
6. Mix the eggs, milk, cheddar cheese shreds, salt, and pepper in a medium bowl.
7. Pour the egg mixture into the pan with the fish and spinach.
8. Pour the egg mixture into the pie crust that has yet to be baked.
9. Bake the salmon and spinach quiche in an oven heated for about 35 to 40 minutes, or until the egg mixture is set and the top is golden brown.

10. Top the salmon and spinach pie with chopped fresh dill and serve it hot.
11. Enjoy your delicious meal!

Turkey And Vegetable Stir-Fry:

Ingredients:

- 1 lb. turkey breast, sliced into strips
- 1 tablespoon cornstarch
- 2 tablespoons soy sauce
- 2 tablespoons vegetable oil
- 1 small onion, chopped
- 1 red bell pepper, seeded and sliced
- 1 green bell pepper, seeded and sliced
- 2 cloves garlic, minced
- 1 cup sliced mushrooms
- Salt and pepper, to taste
- Cooked brown rice for serving

Instructions:

1. Mix cornstarch and soy sauce in a medium bowl with a whisk.
2. Mix the turkey breast strips with the cornstarch and soy sauce in the bowl.
3. In a big skillet, heat vegetable oil over medium-high heat.
4. Add the chopped onion and cook for about 5 minutes or until the onion is transparent.
5. Slice some red and green bell peppers and add them to the pan. Cook for about 2 to 3 minutes or until the peppers are soft.
6. Add chopped garlic and sliced mushrooms to the pan and cook for another 2–3 minutes.
7. Put the turkey breast strips in the pan and cook them for about 5 to 7 minutes or until finished.
8. Add salt and pepper to taste to the stir-fry.
9. Serve the turkey and veggie stir-fry with hot, overcooked brown rice.

10. Enjoy your delicious meal!

Ratatouille With Whole Wheat Couscous:

Ingredients:
- 1 cup whole wheat couscous
- 2 cups vegetable broth
- 2 tablespoons olive oil
- 1 small onion, chopped
- 2 cloves garlic, minced
- 1 red bell pepper, seeded and chopped
- 1 zucchini, sliced
- 1 yellow squash, sliced
- 1 eggplant, peeled and chopped
- 1 can diced tomatoes
- 1 tablespoon chopped fresh basil
- Salt and pepper, to taste
- Grated Parmesan cheese for serving

Instructions:
1. Bring vegetable soup to a boil in a small pot. Stir in the couscous made from whole wheat.
2. Take the pot off the heat and let the couscous soak for about 5 minutes.
3. Use a fork to fluff the couscous, then set it away.
4. Olive oil is heated over medium-high heat in a large pot. Add the chopped onion and cook for about 5 minutes or until the onion is transparent.
5. Put chopped garlic in the pan and cook it for 1 to 2 minutes.
6. Add chopped red bell pepper, yellow squash, zucchini, and chopped eggplant to the pan. Cook the vegetables for about 5–7 minutes or until soft.
7. Add diced canned tomatoes to the pan and season to taste with salt and pepper.

8. Simmer the ratatouille for 10 to 15 minutes or until the flavors have mixed well and the sauce has thickened.
9. Serve the ratatouille over the cooked whole wheat couscous while it is hot.
10. Sprinkle-grated Parmesan cheese on top of the ratatouille, and enjoy your fabulous meal!

Spinach And Ricotta Stuffed Shells:

Ingredients:
- 12 jumbo pasta shells
- 1 tablespoon olive oil
- 1 small onion, chopped
- 2 cloves garlic, minced
- 4 cups fresh baby spinach
- 1 cup ricotta cheese
- 1/2 cup grated Parmesan cheese
- 1 egg
- Salt and pepper, to taste
- 1 can diced tomatoes
- Chopped fresh parsley for serving

Instructions:
1. Follow the directions on the package for cooking jumbo pasta shells in a big pot of salted boiling water. Drain and put away.
2. Olive oil is heated over medium-high heat in a large pot. Add the chopped onion and cook for about 5 minutes or until the onion is transparent.
3. Put chopped garlic in the pan and cook it for 1 to 2 minutes.
4. Add fresh baby spinach to the pan and cook for 2 to 3 minutes, until it wilts.
5. Mix ricotta cheese, chopped Parmesan cheese, an egg, salt, and pepper to taste in a medium bowl.

6. Combine the cooked spinach mixture with the cheese and egg mixture in a mixing bowl. Stir everything until it's all mixed well.
7. Stuff the spinach and ricotta filling into the jumbo shells that have been cooked.
8. Diced tomatoes from a can should be heated over medium heat in a big skillet.
9. Add stuffed shells of pasta to the tomato sauce in the pan.
10. Cover the pan with a lid and simmer the stuffed shells in the tomato sauce for 10 to 15 minutes, until the flavors are well blended, and the bodies are hot.
11. Serve the hot shells filled with spinach and ricotta with chopped fresh parsley on top.
12. Enjoy your delicious meal!

Grilled Veggie Tacos With Avocado Cream:

Ingredients:

- 1 red bell pepper, seeded and sliced
- 1 yellow bell pepper, seeded and sliced
- 1 zucchini, sliced
- 1 yellow squash, sliced
- 1 red onion, sliced
- 2 tablespoons olive oil
- Salt and pepper, to taste
- 8 corn tortillas
- 1 avocado
- 1/2 cup sour cream
- 1 lime, juiced
- Chopped fresh cilantro for serving

Instructions:

1. Set the grill's heat to medium-high.

2. Mix sliced red and yellow bell peppers, zucchini, yellow squash, and red onion with olive oil, salt, and pepper to taste in a big mixing bowl.
3. Grill the vegetables for about 5–7 minutes or until they are browned and soft.
4. Warm the corn tortillas on the grill for 1-2 minutes per side.
5. Use a fork to mash up the avocado in a small bowl.
6. Mix the mashed avocado, sour cream, lime juice, salt, and pepper. Stir everything until it's all mixed well.
7. On each corn tortilla, spread the avocado sauce.
8. Grilled vegetables can be put in each tortilla.
9. Chopped fresh cilantro goes on top of the grilled vegetable tacos.
10. Serve the tacos with avocado sauce while they are still hot.

Baked Chicken And Vegetable Casserole:

Ingredients:

- 1 lb. boneless, skinless chicken breasts, cubed
- 2 tablespoons olive oil
- 1 small onion, chopped
- 2 cloves garlic, minced
- 1 red bell pepper, seeded and chopped
- 1 yellow squash, sliced
- 1 zucchini, sliced
- 1 can diced tomatoes
- Salt and pepper, to taste
- 1/2 cup shredded cheddar cheese
- Chopped fresh parsley for serving

Instructions:

1. Turn oven on to 375°F.

2. Olive oil is heated over medium-high heat in a large pot. Add the chopped onion and cook for about 5 minutes or until the onion is transparent.
3. Put chopped garlic in the pan and cook it for 1 to 2 minutes.
4. Add chopped chicken breasts to the pan and cook for about 5 to 7 minutes or until the meat is no longer pink.
5. Add diced canned tomatoes, chopped red bell pepper, sliced yellow squash, sliced zucchini, and salt and pepper to taste.
6. Everything should be cooked together for about 7 minutes or until the vegetables are soft.
7. Move the chicken and vegetables to a dish for baking.
8. Shred some cheddar cheese and sprinkle it on the chicken and vegetables.
9. Bake the chicken and veggie casserole for 15 to 20 minutes or until the cheese is melted and bubbling.
10. On top of the dish, sprinkle chopped fresh parsley.
11. Serve the baked chicken and veggie casserole while it is still hot, and enjoy your tasty meal.

Chickpea And Kale Stew:

Ingredients:

- 2 tablespoons olive oil
- 1 small onion, chopped
- 2 cloves garlic, minced
- 1 can chickpeas, drained and rinsed
- 1 can diced tomatoes
- 2 cups vegetable broth
- 2 cups chopped kale
- 1 teaspoon ground cumin
- Salt and pepper, to taste
- 1/4 cup chopped fresh parsley for serving

Instructions:

1. Olive oil is heated in a big pot over medium-high heat. Add the chopped onion and cook for about 5 minutes or until the onion is transparent.
2. Add chopped garlic to the pot and cook for 1 to 2 minutes.
3. Add chickpeas that have been rinsed and drained, diced tomatoes from a can, and vegetarian broth to the pot.
4. Add cumin powder, salt, and pepper to taste to the pot.
5. Simmer the stew for 10 to 15 minutes or until the flavors are well mixed.
6. Add the chopped kale to the pot and cook for another 5–7 minutes or until the kale is soft and wilted.
7. Serve the chickpea and kale stew hot, with fresh parsley that has been chopped.
8. Enjoy your delicious meal!

Panko-Crusted Baked Fish With Green Beans:

Ingredients:
- 4 white fish fillets (such as cod or tilapia)
- 1/2 cup all-purpose flour
- 1 egg, beaten
- 1 cup panko bread crumbs
- Salt and pepper, to taste
- 2 tablespoons olive oil
- 1 lb. green beans, trimmed
- 1/4 cup grated Parmesan cheese

Instructions:
1. Turn oven on to 375°F.
2. Put the all-purpose flour, a beaten egg, and panko bread crumbs in three different bowls.
3. Salt and pepper the white fish pieces to your taste.

4. Dip each fish piece in the all-purpose flour, the beaten egg, and the panko bread crumbs. Make sure there is enough coating on each fish.
5. Olive oil is heated over medium-high heat in a large pot.
6. Add the fish pieces coated in panko to the skillet and cook for 2 to 3 minutes per side or until golden brown.
7. Place the fish pieces in a dish for baking.
8. Put green beans trimmed around the fish pieces in the baking dish.
9. Grate some Parmesan cheese and sprinkle it over the green beans.
10. Bake the fish pieces coated in panko and the green beans in an oven that has already been heated for 10 to 15 minutes or until the fish is done and the green beans are soft.
11. Serve the fish and green beans while still hot, and enjoy your tasty meal.

Vegetarian Fajitas With Black Beans And Rice:

Ingredients:
- 1 tablespoon olive oil
- 1 red bell pepper, seeded and sliced
- 1 yellow bell pepper, seeded and sliced
- 1 onion, sliced
- 1 can black beans, drained and rinsed
- 1 tablespoon chili powder
- Salt and pepper, to taste
- 8 flour tortillas
- 1 cup cooked white rice
- Salsa, sour cream, and chopped fresh cilantro for serving

Instructions:

1. Olive oil is heated over medium-high heat in a large pot. Add red and yellow bell pepper slices and onion slices to the pan. Cook the vegetables for about 5–7 minutes or until soft.
2. Add black beans that have been rinsed and drained to the pan. Season to taste with chili powder, salt, and pepper.
3. Cook everything together for another 2–3 minutes or until the black beans are warm.
4. Warm the flour tortillas in a different pan over medium heat for 1 to 2 minutes per side.
5. The black bean and vegetable mix is served with warm flour tacos and cooked white rice.
6. Put salsa, sour cream, and chopped fresh cilantro on the fajitas.
7. Your veggie fajitas with black beans and rice are delicious.

Baked Ziti With Spinach And Mozzarella:

Ingredients:
- 1 lb. ziti pasta
- 2 tablespoons olive oil
- 2 cloves garlic, minced
- 4 cups fresh baby spinach
- 1 can diced tomatoes
- 1 teaspoon dried oregano
- Salt and pepper, to taste
- 2 cups shredded mozzarella cheese
- 1/4 cup grated Parmesan cheese
- Chopped fresh basil for serving

Instructions:
1. Turn oven on to 375°F.
2. Cook ziti according to the directions on the package in a big pot of salted boiling water. Drain and put away.

3. Olive oil is heated over medium-high heat in a large pot. Add chopped garlic and cook for about 1 to 2 minutes.
4. Add fresh baby spinach to the pan and cook for 2 to 3 minutes, until it wilts.
5. Add diced tomatoes from a can to the pan and season to taste with dried oregano, salt, and pepper.
6. Cook everything together for 5–7 minutes or until the tastes are well mixed.
7. Mix the cooked ziti with the tomato and spinach mixture in a big bowl.
8. Shred some mozzarella cheese, cut some Parmesan cheese, and put them in the mixing bowl. Stir everything until it's all mixed well.
9. Move the ziti mixture to a dish for baking.
10. Bake the ziti with spinach and mozzarella in the oven for 15 to 20 minutes or until the cheese is melted and bubbly.
11. On top of the baked ziti, sprinkle chopped fresh basil.
12. Serve the baked ziti with spinach and cheese while it's still hot, and enjoy a tasty meal.

Thai Green Curry With Chicken And Vegetables:

Ingredients:

- 1 lb. boneless, skinless chicken breasts, cubed
- 2 tablespoons green curry paste
- 1 can of coconut milk
- 1 cup chopped mixed vegetables (such as carrots, bell peppers, and zucchini)
- Salt and pepper, to taste
- 1 tablespoon fish sauce
- 1 tablespoon brown sugar
- Juice of 1 lime
- Cooked white rice for serving

Instructions:

1. Green curry paste should be heated over medium-high heat in a big pot. Add cubed chicken breasts to the bank and cook for about 5 to 7 minutes or until the chicken is no longer pink.
2. Salt and pepper to taste, then add chopped mixed veggies to the pot.
3. Pour the coconut milk into the pot and mix it all up.
4. Bring the mixture to a boil, turn down the heat, and cook for 10 to 15 minutes until the vegetables are soft and the flavors have mixed well.
5. Add fish sauce, brown sugar, and lime juice to the pot. Stir everything until it's all mixed well.
6. Serve the Thai green curry with cooked white rice and enjoy your tasty meal.

Pork Tenderloin With Roasted Vegetables:

Ingredients:

- 1 lb. pork tenderloin
- 2 tablespoons olive oil
- Salt and pepper, to taste
- 1 lb. mixed vegetables (such as sweet potatoes, Brussels sprouts, and red onion), chopped
- 2 tablespoons honey
- 2 tablespoons balsamic vinegar
- 1 tablespoon Dijon mustard
- 1 teaspoon dried thyme

Instructions:

1. Turn oven on to 400°F.
2. Rub olive oil into pork chops and add salt and pepper to taste.
3. Mix chopped veggies, olive oil, salt, and pepper in a large bowl.

4. Move the pork tenderloin and mixed veggies to a dish for baking.
5. Put the pork tenderloin and mixed vegetables in the oven for about 25 to 30 minutes, or until the pork is done and the vegetables are soft.
6. Whisk together the honey, balsamic vinegar, Dijon mustard, and dried thyme in a small bowl.
7. Brush the pork tenderloin and veggies with the honey mixture.
8. Put everything back in the baking dish and the oven for another 5–7 minutes or until the honey glaze is browned.
9. Serve the pork tenderloin with the roasted veggies while they are still hot, and enjoy your tasty meal.

White Bean And Kale Soup With Whole Wheat Bread:

Ingredients:

- 2 tablespoons olive oil
- 1 onion, chopped
- 2 cloves garlic, minced
- 2 cans white beans, drained and rinsed
- 4 cups vegetable broth
- 2 cups chopped kale
- 1 teaspoon dried oregano
- Salt and pepper, to taste
- Whole wheat bread for serving

Instructions:

1. Olive oil is heated in a big pot over medium-high heat. Add the chopped onion and cook for about 5 minutes or until the onion is transparent.
2. Add chopped garlic to the pot and cook for 1 to 2 minutes.
3. Add white beans, rinsed and drained, and veggie broth to the pot.

4. Add dried oregano, salt, and pepper to taste the soup.
5. Simmer the soup for 10 to 15 minutes or until all tastes have mixed well.
6. Add the chopped kale to the pot and cook for another 5–7 minutes or until the kale is soft and wilted.
7. White bean and kale soup should be served hot with whole wheat bread.
8. Enjoy your delicious meal!

Shrimp And Vegetable Coconut Curry:

Ingredients:

- 1 lb. shrimp, peeled and deveined
- 2 tablespoons olive oil
- 1 onion, chopped
- 2 cloves garlic, minced
- 2 bell peppers, chopped
- 1 zucchini, chopped
- 1 can of coconut milk
- 1 tablespoon curry powder
- Salt and pepper, to taste
- Cooked white rice for serving

Instructions:

1. Olive oil is heated over medium-high heat in a large pot. Add the chopped onion and cook for about 5 minutes or until the onion is transparent.
2. Put chopped garlic in the pan and cook it for 1 to 2 minutes.
3. Add bell peppers and zucchini that have been cut up to the pan. Everything should be cooked together for about 7 minutes or until the vegetables are soft.
4. Add shrimp that have been peeled and deveined to the pan. Cook for another 2–3 minutes or until the shrimp turns pink and is done.
5. Curry powder, salt, and pepper, to taste, can be added to the coconut milk in the pan.

6. Simmer the curry for 10 to 15 minutes or until all the flavors have mixed well.
7. Serve the shrimp and vegetables in the hot coconut soup with a side of cooked white rice.
8. Enjoy your delicious meal!

Vegetarian Lentil And Quinoa Chili:

Ingredients:

- 1 tablespoon olive oil
- 1 onion, chopped
- 2 cloves garlic, minced
- 2 bell peppers, chopped
- 2 cans diced tomatoes
- 1 can black beans, drained and rinsed
- 1 can kidney beans, drained and rinsed
- 1/2 cup uncooked quinoa
- 1/2 cup uncooked lentils
- 2 tablespoons chili powder
- 1 teaspoon ground cumin
- Salt and pepper, to taste
- Shredded cheddar cheese, sour cream, and chopped fresh cilantro for serving

Instructions:

1. Olive oil is heated in a big pot over medium-high heat. Add the chopped onion and cook for about 5 minutes or until the onion is transparent.
2. Add chopped garlic to the pot and cook for 1 to 2 minutes.
3. Add chopped bell peppers, diced tomatoes from a can, black beans that have been rinsed and drained, kidney beans that have been exhausted, uncooked rice, and uncooked lentils to the pot.
4. Add chili powder, ground cumin, salt, and pepper to taste the soup.
5. Add enough water to cover everything in the pot.

6. Bring the chili to a boil, boil the heat, and cook for 30–40 minutes until the lentils and quinoa are soft and the flavors have mixed well.
7. Serve the hot lentil and quinoa soup with cheddar cheese shreds, sour cream, and chopped fresh cilantro on top.
8. Enjoy your delicious meal!

Lemon And Dill Baked Tilapia:

Ingredients:

- 4 tilapia fillets
- 2 tablespoons olive oil
- Juice of 1 lemon
- 1 teaspoon dried dill
- Salt and pepper, to taste

Instructions:

1. Turn oven on to 375°F.
2. Fillets of tilapia should be put in a baking dish.
3. Sprinkle the tilapia pieces with olive oil and lemon juice.
4. The tilapia pieces can be seasoned to taste with dried dill, salt, and pepper.
5. Bake the tilapia in an oven that has been warm for 15 to 20 minutes or until the fish is cooked and flakes easily with a fork.
6. Serve the baked fish with lemon and dill while it's hot, and enjoy your tasty meal.

Beef And Vegetable Stir-Fry With Brown Rice:

Ingredients:

- 1 lb. meat, sliced
- 2 tablespoons olive oil

- 1 onion, sliced
- 2 bell peppers, sliced
- 2 carrots, sliced
- 1 broccoli, chopped
- 1/4 cup soy sauce
- 1 tablespoon cornstarch
- 1 tablespoon honey
- 1 teaspoon ground ginger
- Salt and pepper, to taste
- Cooked brown rice for serving

Instructions:

1. Olive oil should be heated in a big skillet or wok over medium-high heat. Add the sliced meat and cook for about 5–7 minutes, until it's browned on all sides.
2. Take the meat out of the pan and set it aside.
3. Put chopped onion, bell peppers, carrots, and broccoli in the pan. Everything should be cooked together for about 7 minutes or until the vegetables are soft.
4. Mix the soy sauce, cornstarch, honey, ground ginger, salt, and pepper in a small bowl.
5. Pour the soy sauce mixture over the vegetables already in the pan.
6. Add the beef back to the pan and stir until the sauce has thickened and all the ingredients are well mixed.
7. Serve the stir-fried beef and vegetables hot, with a side of cooked brown rice.
8. Enjoy your delicious meal!

Turkey Meatloaf With Mashed Sweet Potatoes:

Ingredients:

- 1 lb. ground turkey
- 1/2 cup breadcrumbs
- 1/2 cup grated Parmesan cheese
- 1 egg, beaten

- 1 onion, chopped
- 2 cloves garlic, minced
- 1 teaspoon dried thyme
- Salt and pepper, to taste
- 4 sweet potatoes, peeled and chopped
- 1/4 cup milk
- 2 tablespoons butter

Instructions:

1. Turn oven on to 375°F.
2. Mix ground turkey, breadcrumbs, grated Parmesan cheese, an egg that has been beaten, chopped onion, minced garlic, dried thyme, salt, and pepper in a big bowl.
3. Mix all of the ingredients until they're well blended.
4. Put the filling for the meatloaf into a loaf pan.
5. The turkey meatloaf needs to be cooked in a hot oven for about 45 to 50 minutes until the middle is no longer pink.
6. While the meatloaf is cooking, boil the chopped sweet potatoes in a big pot of water for 10-15 minutes until soft.
7. Drain the sweet potatoes, then mash them with milk and butter until they are smooth and creamy.
8. Hot mashed sweet potatoes should be served with the turkey meatballs.
9. Enjoy your delicious meal!

Spicy Tofu And Broccoli Stir-Fry:

Ingredients:

- 1 lb. firm tofu, pressed and cubed
- 2 tablespoons cornstarch
- 2 tablespoons soy sauce
- 2 tablespoons vegetable oil
- 2 cloves garlic, minced
- 1 tablespoon grated ginger
- 1/4 teaspoon red pepper flakes

- 1 onion, sliced
- 2 cups broccoli florets
- 2 tablespoons hoisin sauce
- Salt and pepper, to taste
- Cooked brown rice for serving

Instructions:

1. Mix the cornstarch and soy sauce in a small bowl with a whisk.
2. Put cubed tofu in the bowl and toss it with the cornstarch mixture until well covered.
3. Heat vegetable oil over medium-high heat in a big pan or wok. Put red pepper flakes, chopped garlic, and grated ginger into the pan. Cook for about a minute or two or until the smell is pleasant.
4. Add sliced onion to the pan and cook for about 5 minutes or until the onion is transparent.
5. Add the broccoli pieces and cook everything together for about 7 minutes or until the broccoli is soft.
6. Put the tofu in the pan and stir everything until the tofu is warm.
7. Pour the hoisin sauce into the pan with the tofu and vegetables.
8. Add salt and pepper to taste to the stir-fry.
9. Spicy tofu and broccoli stir-fry should be served hot with a side of cooked brown rice.
10. Enjoy your delicious meal!

Baked Eggplant Parmesan With Whole Wheat Spaghetti:

Ingredients:

- 1 large eggplant, sliced
- 1/2 cup breadcrumbs
- 1/4 cup grated Parmesan cheese
- 1 egg, beaten
- 2 cups marinara sauce

- 2 cups shredded mozzarella cheese
- Salt and pepper, to taste
- Whole wheat spaghetti for serving

Instructions:

1. Turn oven on to 375°F.
2. Dip sliced eggplant in an egg that has been beaten, and then coat them with breadcrumbs mixed with Parmesan cheese.
3. Put the slices of eggplant on a baking sheet covered with parchment paper.
4. Bake the eggplant slices in the oven for about 25 to 30 minutes or until they are soft and crispy.
5. Take the eggplant slices out of the oven and cool down for a few minutes.
6. Spread some tomato sauce on the bottom of a 9x13-inch baking dish.
7. Cover the marinara sauce with a layer of eggplant pieces.
8. Shreds of mozzarella cheese should be put on top of the eggplant pieces.
9. Repeat the stages of marinara sauce, eggplant slices, and shredded mozzarella cheese until all ingredients are used.
10. Salt and pepper the eggplant Parmesan to your taste.
11. Bake the eggplant parmesan in the oven for 30 to 40 minutes or until the cheese is melted and bubbly.
12. Serve the baked eggplant Parmesan while it is hot, along with whole wheat spaghetti.
13. Enjoy your delicious meal!

Chicken And Vegetable Kebabs With Tzatziki Sauce:

Ingredients:

- 1 lb. chicken breasts, cut into cubes
- 2 bell peppers, cut into chunks
- 2 zucchinis, cut into chunks
- 1 onion, cut into chunks
- 1/4 cup olive oil
- 2 tablespoons lemon juice
- 2 teaspoons dried oregano
- Salt and pepper, to taste
- Wooden skewers soaked in water for at least 30 minutes
- Tzatziki sauce for serving

Instructions:

1. Whisk together olive oil, lemon juice, dried oregano, salt, and pepper in a small bowl.
2. Using wooden skewers, alternate chicken cubes, bell pepper chunks, zucchini chunks, and onion chunks.
3. The olive oil blend is used to paint the kebabs.
4. Set the grill's heat to medium-high.
5. Turn the kebabs every few minutes for 10 to 12 minutes, or until the chicken is done and the vegetables are soft.
6. Serve the chicken and veggie kebabs while still hot, with a side of tzatziki sauce.
7. Enjoy your delicious meal!

Seared Tuna With Sesame Brown Rice:

Ingredients:

- 4 tuna steaks
- 2 tablespoons sesame oil
- 1 tablespoon soy sauce
- 1 tablespoon honey
- 1 tablespoon rice vinegar
- Salt and pepper, to taste
- 2 cups cooked brown rice
- 2 tablespoons sesame seeds

Instructions:

1. Whisk together sesame oil, soy sauce, honey, rice vinegar, salt, and pepper in a small bowl.
2. Spread the sesame oil mixture on the tuna pieces.
3. Heat a big skillet over high heat.
4. Add the tuna steaks to the pan and cook for 1 to 2 minutes on each side until they are browned outside but still pink in the middle.
5. Toast sesame seeds in a different pan over medium heat until lightly browned.
6. Seared tuna steaks should be served hot with cooked brown rice and sesame seeds that have been warmed.
7. Enjoy your delicious meal!

Chicken And Mushroom Risotto With Spinach:

Ingredients:

- 1 lb. chicken breasts, cut into bite-sized pieces
- 1 onion, chopped
- 2 cups mushrooms, sliced
- 2 cloves garlic, minced
- 1 cup Arborio rice
- 1/2 cup white wine
- 4 cups chicken broth

- 2 cups fresh spinach
- 1/4 cup grated Parmesan cheese
- 2 tablespoons butter
- Salt and pepper, to taste

Instructions:

1. In a big pan or Dutch oven, melt 1 tablespoon of butter over medium-high heat.
2. Add the chicken pieces to the pan and cook for about 5 to 7 minutes or until they are browned on all sides. Take the chicken out of the pan and put it away.
3. Add chopped onion, cut mushrooms, and minced garlic to the pan. Everything should be cooked together for about 7 minutes or until the vegetables are soft.
4. Add the Arborio rice to the pan and cook it for about 1 to 2 minutes while turning it all the time.
5. Pour the white wine into the pan and stir until all of the wine is used up.
6. Pour the chicken broth in slowly, turning often, and cook everything together for about 20 to 25 minutes, or until the rice is soft and the liquid has been absorbed.
7. Mix in cooked chicken bits, fresh spinach, grated Parmesan cheese, and 1 tablespoon of butter.
8. Salt and pepper the rice to your taste.
9. The chicken and vegetable risotto should be served hot.
10. Enjoy your delicious meal!

Spicy Black Bean And Vegetable Quinoa:

Ingredients:

- 1 cup quinoa
- 2 cups vegetable broth
- 1 tablespoon olive oil
- 1 onion, chopped
- 2 cloves garlic, minced

- 1 red bell pepper, chopped
- 1 zucchini, chopped
- 1 jalapeno pepper, seeded and chopped
- 1 can black beans, drained and rinsed
- 2 tablespoons tomato paste
- 1 teaspoon cumin
- Salt and pepper, to taste

Instructions:
1. Rinse quinoa with cold water and then let it drain.
2. Mix the quinoa and the veggie broth in a medium saucepan. Bring to a boil over high heat, then reduce heat to low and simmer for about 15 to 20 minutes, or until the quinoa is cooked and the liquid is absorbed.
3. Olive oil is heated over medium-high heat in a large pot. Put chopped onion, minced garlic, red bell pepper, zucchini, and jalapeno pepper in the pan. Everything should be cooked together for about 7 minutes or until the vegetables are soft.
4. Add the black beans, rinsed and drained, tomato paste, cumin, salt, and pepper to the pan. Stir everything until it's all well mixed.
5. Add the cooked quinoa to the pan and stir until it is warm and the sauce has covered it well.
6. Spicy black beans and veggie quinoa should be served hot.
7. Enjoy your delicious meal!

Grilled Swordfish With Mediterranean Salsa:

Ingredients:

- 4 swordfish steaks
- 2 tablespoons olive oil
- Salt and pepper, to taste
- For the salsa:
- 1 cup cherry tomatoes, chopped
- 1/2 cup kalamata olives, chopped
- 1/2 cup red onion, chopped
- 2 tablespoons capers, chopped
- 2 tablespoons fresh parsley, chopped
- 1 tablespoon fresh lemon juice
- 2 tablespoons olive oil
- Salt and pepper, to taste

Instructions:

1. Set the grill's heat to medium-high.
2. Salt and pepper the swordfish steaks after brushing them with olive oil.
3. The swordfish steaks need 3–4 minutes on each side of the grill or until they are cooked through.
4. Mix cherry tomatoes, kalamata olives, red onion, capers, fresh parsley, lemon juice, olive oil, salt, and pepper in a small mixing bowl.
5. Serve the swordfish steaks cooked hot with Mediterranean salsa on top.
6. Enjoy your delicious meal!

Stuffed Acorn Squash With Wild Rice And Mushrooms:

Ingredients:

- 2 acorn squashes, halved and seeded
- 1 cup wild rice, rinsed and drained
- 2 cups vegetable broth
- 2 tablespoons olive oil
- 1 onion, chopped
- 2 cloves garlic, minced
- 2 cups mushrooms, sliced
- 2 cups fresh spinach
- 1/4 cup grated Parmesan cheese
- Salt and pepper, to taste

Instructions:

1. Turn oven on to 375°F.
2. Cut acorn squash in half and remove the seeds. Place the cut side up on a baking sheet lined with parchment paper.
3. Bake the acorn squashes for 30 to 35 minutes or until soft.
4. Mix wild rice and veggie broth in a medium saucepan. Bring to a boil over high heat, then boil to low and simmer for about 30 to 40 minutes, or until the rice is done and the liquid has been absorbed.
5. Olive oil is heated over medium-high heat in a large pot. Put some chopped onion and sliced garlic in the pan. Cook for about a minute or two or until the smell is pleasant.
6. Slice some mushrooms and add them to the pan. Cook for 5–7 minutes or until they are soft.
7. Add fresh spinach to the pan and cook it for about 1-2 minutes, until it wilts.
8. Cook some wild rice and grate some Parmesan cheese. Stir everything until it's all well mixed.
9. Add salt and pepper to taste the stuffing.

10. Put the stuffing into the acorn squash halves that have been baked.
11. When the oven is hot, bake the stuffed acorn squashes for 10 to 15 minutes or until the filling is hot.
12. The stuffed acorn squash should be served hot.
13. Enjoy your delicious meal!

CHAPTER:8 SNACK RECIPES

Banana And Almond Butter Toast:

Ingredients:

- 2 slices of whole wheat bread
- 2 tablespoons almond butter
- 1 banana, sliced
- 1 tablespoon honey

Instructions:

1. The slices of whole wheat bread should be toasted until they are crisp.
2. On each piece of toasted bread, spread 1 tablespoon of almond butter.
3. Put slices of banana on top of the almond butter.
4. Honey should be poured over the bananas.
5. The banana and almond butter toast should be served hot.
6. Enjoy your delicious meal!

Greek Yogurt With Honey And Mixed Berries:

Ingredients:
1. Greek yogurt, 1 cup
2. 1/2 cup of berries like blueberries, raspberries, and strawberries mixed.
3. 1 spoonful of honey
4. Instructions:
5. Mix Greek yogurt, mixed berries, and honey in a small bowl.
6. Stir everything until it's all well mixed.
7. Greek yogurt with honey and a mix of berries should be served cold.
8. Enjoy your delicious meal!

Homemade Trail Mix With Nuts, Seeds, And Dried Fruit:

Ingredients:
- 1/2 cup almonds
- 1/2 cup cashews
- 1/2 cup pumpkin seeds
- 1/2 cup dried cranberries
- 1/2 cup raisins

Instructions:
1. Mix almonds, cashews, pumpkin seeds, dried cranberries, and raisins in a medium bowl.
2. Stir everything until it's all well mixed.
3. Split the trail mix into small bags that can be used as snacks.
4. Put the homemade trail mix in a jar that won't let air in.
5. Enjoy your delicious snack!

Vegetable Sticks With Hummus:

Ingredients:

- Carrots, celery, and bell peppers cut into sticks
- 1 cup of hummus

Instructions:

1. Wash the food and cut it into sticks.
2. Use hummus as a dip for the vegetable sticks.
3. Enjoy your delicious snack!

Cottage Cheese And Pineapple:

Ingredients:

- 1 cup of low-fat cottage cheese
- 1 cup of diced pineapple

Instructions:

1. Cottage cheese should be put in a bowl.
2. Diced pineapple goes on top.
3. Cottage cheese and pineapple can be a snack or part of your breakfast.
4. Enjoy your delicious snack!

Roasted Chickpeas With Spices:

Ingredients:

- 1 can of chickpeas, drained and rinsed
- 1 tablespoon olive oil
- 1 teaspoon cumin
- 1 teaspoon smoked paprika
- 1/2 teaspoon garlic powder
- Salt and pepper to taste

Instructions:

1. Turn oven on to 400°F.
2. Drain, rinse, and pat dry the chickpeas.

3. Mix chickpeas, olive oil, cumin, smoked paprika, garlic powder, salt, and pepper in a medium bowl. Stir everything together until the chickpeas are well covered with the spice blend.
4. Spread the chickpeas in a single layer on a parchment paper-lined baking sheet.
5. The chickpeas should be roasted in the oven for 20 to 25 minutes or until crispy and golden brown.
6. As a snack, serve the roasted chickpeas.
7. Enjoy your delicious snack!

Whole Wheat Crackers And Cheese:

Ingredients:
- Whole wheat crackers
- Cheddar cheese, sliced

Instructions:
1. Put the crackers made from whole wheat on a dish to serve.
2. Set the slices of cheddar cheese on top of the crackers.
3. Serve the cheese and whole wheat crackers as a snack.
4. Enjoy your delicious snack!

Apple Slices With Peanut Butter:

Ingredients:

- Apples, sliced
- Peanut butter

Instructions:

1. Wash apples and cut them into pieces.
2. Use peanut butter as a dip for apple pieces.
3. Enjoy your delicious snack!

Edamame With Sea Salt:

Ingredients:

- 1 cup frozen edamame
- 1 teaspoon sea salt

Instructions:

1. Bring some water to a boil in a pot.
2. Add the edamame and cook it for 5 to 7 minutes or until soft.
3. Place the drained edamame in a bowl.
4. Add sea salt to the edamame and mix it up nicely.
5. Serve the edamame as a snack or starter with sea salt.
6. Enjoy your delicious snack!

Smoked Salmon And Cream Cheese On Whole Grain Crackers:

Ingredients:
- Whole grain crackers
- Smoked salmon, sliced
- Cream cheese

Instructions:
1. Spread cream cheese on each bread made with whole grains.
2. On each piece of bread, put a slice of smoked salmon.
3. Put the smoked salmon and cream cheese on whole-grain bread as a snack or starter.
4. Enjoy your delicious snack!

Dark Chocolate Covered Almonds:

Ingredients:

- 1 cup almonds
- 1 cup dark chocolate chips

Instructions:

1. Put parchment paper on a baking sheet.
2. Use a double pot or microwave to melt the dark chocolate chips.
3. Stir the nuts into the melted chocolate until they are all covered.
4. Put the chocolate-covered nuts on the parchment paper with a spoon.
5. Let the nuts with chocolate on them cool down and harden.
6. Once the chocolate-covered almonds have set and cooled, take them off the parchment paper.
7. Serve the almonds that are wrapped in dark chocolate as a snack.
8. Enjoy your delicious snack!

Mixed Berry And Yogurt Parfait:

Ingredients:

- 1 cup plain Greek yogurt
- 1 cup mixed berries (such as blueberries, raspberries, and strawberries)
- 1/4 cup granola

Instructions:

1. Stack Greek yogurt, mixed berries, and granola in a small glass.
2. Keep putting things on top of each other until the glass is full.

3. Serve the yogurt and mixed berries cold.
4. Have fun with your tasty snack or meal!

Oatmeal Raisin Cookies Made With Whole Wheat Flour:

Ingredients:
- 1 1/2 cups whole wheat flour
- 1/2 teaspoon baking soda
- 1/2 teaspoon ground cinnamon
- 1/2 teaspoon salt
- 1/2 cup unsalted butter, softened
- 1/2 cup brown sugar
- 1/4 cup granulated sugar
- 2 eggs
- 1 teaspoon vanilla extract
- 1 1/2 cups rolled oats
- 1 cup raisins

Instructions:
1. Turn oven on to 350°F.
2. Mix the whole wheat flour, baking soda, ground cinnamon, and salt in a medium bowl.
3. In a different large bowl, beat the butter, brown sugar, and white sugar together until they are light and fluffy.
4. Beat well after adding the eggs and vanilla extract to the butter mixture.
5. Mix well as you slowly add the dry ingredients to the wet ingredients.
6. Mix in the raisins and rolled oats.
7. Put spoonfuls of the dough on a baking sheet covered with parchment paper.
8. Bake the oatmeal-raisin cookies for 10 to 12 minutes or until golden brown.
9. Take the cookies out of the oven and let them cool on a wire rack.

10. The oatmeal raisin cookies can be served as a snack or a dessert.
11. Enjoy your tasty snack or sweet treat!

Fruit Salad With Honey-Lime Dressing:

Ingredients:

- 2 cups mixed fruit (such as strawberries, blueberries, raspberries, and sliced kiwi)
- 2 tablespoons honey
- 1 tablespoon lime juice
- 1/4 teaspoon ground cinnamon

Instructions:

1. Mix honey, lime juice, and ground cinnamon in a small bowl.
2. Mix different kinds of fruit in a big bowl.
3. Pour the honey-lime sauce over the fruit and toss it well to coat it.
4. The fruit salad with the honey-lime sauce should be served cold.
5. Enjoy your tasty snack or sweet treat!

Chia Seed Pudding With Fresh Fruit:

Ingredients:

- 1/4 cup chia seeds
- 1 cup almond milk
- 1 tablespoon honey
- 1/2 teaspoon vanilla extract
- 1/2 cup mixed fresh fruit (such as sliced strawberries, blueberries, and raspberries)

Instructions:

1. Mix the chia seeds, almond milk, honey, and vanilla extract in a medium bowl.
2. Stir everything together until it's all mixed well.

3. Put the bowl in the fridge for at least 2 hours or overnight, covered with plastic wrap.
4. Before you serve the pudding, stir it.
5. Fresh fruit is put on top of the chia seed stew.
6. Fresh fruit goes well with the cold chia seed pudding.
7. Have fun with your tasty snack or meal!

Baked Apples With Cinnamon And Walnuts:

Ingredients:

- 2 apples, cored and sliced
- 1/4 cup walnuts, chopped
- 1 teaspoon ground cinnamon
- 1 tablespoon honey
- 1 tablespoon unsalted butter

Instructions:

1. Turn oven on to 375°F.
2. Mix chopped walnuts, cinnamon powder, and honey in a small bowl.
3. Put some of the walnut mixture in the middle of each apple slice.
4. Put the apples that have been stuffed in a baking dish.
5. Spread plain butter on top of the stuffed apples.
6. Bake the apples for about 25 to 30 minutes or until soft and light golden.
7. Serve the apples that have been baked with cinnamon and hot nuts.
8. Enjoy your tasty snack or sweet treat!

Chocolate Avocado Mousse:

Ingredients:

- 2 ripe avocados, pitted and peeled
- 1/4 cup unsweetened cocoa powder

- 1/4 cup honey
- 1/4 cup almond milk
- 1 teaspoon vanilla extract

Instructions:
1. Blend or process avocados in a food processor or blender until they are smooth.
2. Blend the chocolate powder, honey, almond milk, and vanilla extract.
3. Mix everything until it's smooth and creamy.
4. Put the chocolate avocado mousse on small plates for serving.
5. Put the mousse in the fridge for at least 30 minutes to cool it down.
6. The chocolate avocado mousse should be served cold.
7. Enjoy your delicious dessert!

Angel Food Cake With Fresh Berries:

Ingredients:
- 1 package angel food cake mix
- 1 cup mixed fresh berries (such as strawberries, blueberries, and raspberries)
- Whipped cream (optional)

Instructions:
1. Turn oven on to 350°F.
2. Follow the steps on the box to make the angel food cake mix.
3. Pour the cake batter into a tube pan that has yet to be greased.
4. Bake the angel food cake in a preheated oven for 35 to 40 minutes, or until a toothpick in the middle of the cake comes out clean.
5. Take the cake out of the oven and let it cool.
6. Cut the angel food cake into pieces and serve with fresh berries.

7. If you want, you can put whipped cream on top of the angel food cake.
8. Enjoy your delicious dessert!

Ricotta And Orange Stuffed Dates:

Ingredients:

- 8 dates, pitted
- 1/4 cup ricotta cheese
- 1 tablespoon honey
- Zest of 1 orange

Instructions:

1. Mix the ricotta cheese, honey, and orange juice in a small bowl.
2. Stuff the ricotta mixture into the middle of each date.
3. Dates stuffed with ricotta and orange can be a snack or a dessert.
4. Enjoy your tasty snack or sweet treat!

Frozen Banana And Peanut Butter Bites:

Ingredients:

- 2 ripe bananas, peeled and sliced
- 1/4 cup creamy peanut butter
- 1/4 cup chocolate chips

Instructions:

1. Put parchment paper on a baking sheet.
2. On one side of each banana slice, spreadPut a second banana slice on top of the peanut butter.
3. To make a banana and pea slice on top.
4. Put the banana and peanut butter bites on the baking sheet that has been made ready.
5. Use the microwave or a double pot to melt the chocolate chips.

6. Pour melted chocolate over the peanut butter and banana bites.
7. Put the banana and peanut butter bites in the freezer for at least half an hour.
8. Cold is the best way to eat the frozen banana and peanut butter bites.
9. Enjoy your tasty snack or sweet treat!

Conclusion:

In conclusion, low blood pressure is a condition that can be managed through a healthy diet that is low in sodium, high in potassium, and includes healthy fats. A balanced diet with plenty of fruits, vegetables, whole grains, lean proteins, and healthy fats can help support cardiovascular health and manage low blood pressure. A diet rich in potassium can help offset the adverse effects of sodium on blood pressure, while healthy fats can help support heart health and manage weight.

Making small and sustainable dietary changes can effectively manage low blood pressure. For example, reducing processed foods, increasing the intake of fresh fruits and vegetables, and limiting sodium intake can be helpful. Additionallypotassium-rich foods, such as bananas, sweet potatoes, and spinach can effectively manage low blood pressure. Healthy fats found in foods such as nuts, seeds, fatty fish, and avocado can also be beneficial in managing low blood pressure.

Working with a healthcare provider to develop a personalized plan for managing low blood pressure and monitoring any dietary changes is essential. While lifestyle modifications such as a healthy diet and physical activity can effectively manage low blood pressure, medication may also be necessary for some individuals. A combination of medication and lifestyle modifications can be the most effective way to manage low blood pressure.

A balanced and healthy diet is essential for managing low blood pressure and supporting overall health and well-being. Individuals with low blood pressure can help support cardiovascular health and reduce the risk of chronic diseases by making gradual and sustainable changes to one's diet and lifestyle.

THE END

Printed in Great Britain
by Amazon

55064386R00086